UNSPOKEN WORD

ONE MOMENT WITH *Jesus* CHANGES EVERYTHING

WRITTEN BY ANGELA O'NEILL

What People Are Saying

Angela masterfully brings the story of Pilate to life, capturing the weight of his decision in a way that feels deeply personal. The tension, the emotion, and the struggle between fear and truth make you feel like you're right there in the moment. But beyond just storytelling, this chapter stirs something more—it invites reflection on our own response to Jesus and how that response is ultimately an act of WORSHIP. Angela's creative approach doesn't just retell scripture; it draws you in, challenges your perspective, and points you back to the heart of worship—seeing Jesus for who He truly is and responding in surrender. – **Aaron Crane, Worship Pastor at Cornerstone Community Church**

Angela O'Neill is a gifted author who brings the stories of the Bible to life through the eyes of its characters. With a God-given ability to illuminate unforeseen details and provide exquisite insight, she invites readers into transformative encounters with Jesus. Her storytelling takes readers as if they are in the scene themselves, experiencing the depth, emotion, and power of each moment. Through her vivid and inspirational writing, Scripture becomes more personal, tangible, and alive. - **Jayme Elizabeth, She Speaks Life Podcast Host.**

Angela doesn't just tell a story—she invites you into it. With every page, you feel the weight of real pain and the wonder of Jesus' grace as if you were living it yourself. Her writing is both beautifully creative and theologically rich, making truth come alive in a way that lingers long after you've finished reading. – **Dallas Viva, Young Adults Pastor, Mariners Church**

Angela O'Neill masterfully brings the Bible's well-known characters to life, revealing their humanity in a way that resonates deeply. Through her poetic words she breathes life into these people, reminding us that they, too, once walked this Earth, just like us. For instance, the leper's story becomes a vivid experience of pain, isolation, and sorrow, conveyed so powerfully that we can almost feel his suffering. Like the leper, we all long for a moment with Jesus—to hear His voice, to find healing, and to be comforted by His love. *Unspoken Word* allows us to encounter Jesus through the stories of these characters and their life-changing experiences with the Savior. It's a beautiful piece of art, expressed through compelling stories and heartfelt artistic words. I can't wait for more readers to immerse themselves in this transformative book! – **Tim Lukei – Executive Director/Founder of Maverick River Collective**

Dear Jon,

Thank you for believing in me!

Thank you for giving me space to "step out of the boat" and answer "yes" to this call!

Thank you for supporting me every step of the way!

Thank you for listening to all of the stories, with all the exclamation points!

I love you!

Contents

The Prologue

—

My love of storytelling began early, rooted in my mom's bedtime story routine. I can still clearly picture the books and their illustrations. I loved listening intently to these bedtime stories, but when I became old enough to read, I began wanting to be the one reading the stories. I wanted to be the storyteller. The love of storytelling quite literally might be my oldest memory. Little did I know then that this love would become a passion and life purpose to tell stories for God's glory.

This book is a compilation of my journey as a storyteller. From performer to director to writer, storytelling is at its root. As a performer, I can not wait to get on stage. A performer's job is to portray a character, respond as the character, know the cues for the character, and see the world on stage through the character's eyes. It is a laser-focused role as a storyteller.

As a Director, I see the relationships between every person on the stage. The intention of each character, no matter how big or small a part, makes a difference in creating the proper interpretation. The director looks at the story's entirety, from character relationships to setting, lighting cues, every entrance and exit...the list goes on, ensuring every detail tells the story dynamically.

As a writer, each detail matters so that everyone in the company understands the intention. Clarity is key. Detailed stage descriptions, character analysis, and punctuation make a big difference in ensuring that the intention and intended interpretation occur, even if the writer is not in the room.

So here we are at the intersection of these three storytelling methods. Each chapter is a scene/character study of an individual story in scripture. Accompanying each chapter is an original dramatic interpretation. The interpretations provide possible subtext and dialogue for the players in the scene. The key word here is "possible". Each dramatic interpretation is based on scripture and extensive biblical and historical research. The dramatic interpretations intend to bring the stories to life. They are not to be taken as exact representations or replacements of scripture. Hopefully, these pieces will provoke thought and reflection on the scriptures themselves and help us remember and consider that the people we read about in the Bible were real; they lived experiences we now get to read about.

The specific characters chosen had at least one physical encounter with Jesus, each encounter unique, and each person's response differed. The impact of testimonies, both then and now, is tremendous. I hope we learn from these varying encounters, experiences, and perspectives and that each of us draws closer to Jesus through the details of the stories. It is then up to us how we respond. Writing this book has helped me to stop, observe the details, reflect, and process, ultimately leading me to understand and experience Jesus on a deeper level. I hope the same is true for you!

How to Read

There is no right or wrong way to read this book, but here are some helpful tools to help you get started.

- This book can be used as a group experience or individually. If used in a group, take a chapter a week to study and come back as a group to discuss. If you want to add a little drama, allow each person to choose a character to read or perform out loud. Embrace the art and experience the stories.

- The intentional breakdown of each chapter uses theatrical terminology.

  - **The Scripture**—Each chapter begins with Scripture, which is the foundation of this book. Everything else simply points back to the word of God.

  - **At Rise**—The opening words of a script describing what is happening on the stage as the curtain rises. The "At Rise" in this book provides a look at the setting and any information that might be helpful leading up to this moment.

- **The Scene**—Plays are typically divided into two acts, maybe three if it's a Shakespearean performance. A compilation of scenes creates an act. In this book, the scene provides a dramatic interpretation from the perspective of the person encountering Jesus.

- **The Story**—The story provides details, character analysis, and pertinent information to help us fully understand the depth and meaning of each encounter with Jesus.

- **The Backstory**—In this section of each chapter, I will share a personal backstory. It's a chance to add a small part of my story, process, thoughts, or inspiration.

- **The Scene Study**—This section allows you to consider the chapter and analyze what you have read, providing space to reflect and delve deeper.

- **The Senses**—The last activity will activate the senses. It allows you to engage with the story tangibly, opening up creativity to connect with the Creator.

The Cover Art

In my years directing the Mariners Church Arts Ministry, I had the privilege of cultivating friendships with some amazing artists. Dianna

Mordin, is one of those artists. The cover is inspired by one of the galleries curated for the lent season entitled *Beauty From Ashes*. The gallery displayed various pieces of art created by artists with ash. Dianna made a piece inspired by the story of Peter walking on water, with Peter's hand reaching up. As my mind swirled with thoughts, I asked Dianna if she would create the cover but with an arm reaching down with a nail scar. The image represents two stories in the book: Peter walking on water and Thomas seeing the scars of the resurrected Jesus. In reality, though, the image represents Jesus' love and pursuit of all of us. The scars are for everyone; He is there for everyone, and He loves everyone. Look back at the art and answer these questions we would ask at the Mariners Arts Gatherings: What do you see? What do you feel? What do you hear (what is God saying to you)?

Chapter I

The Ordinary

The Scripture

Luke 1: 26 - 38 (CSB)

26 In the sixth month, the angel Gabriel was sent by God to a town in Galilee called Nazareth, 27 to a virgin engaged to a man named Joseph, of the house of David. The virgin's name was Mary. 28 And the angel came to her and said, "Greetings, favored woman! The Lord is with you." 29 But she was deeply troubled by this statement, wondering what kind of greeting this could be. 30 Then the angel told her, "Do not be afraid, Mary, for you have found favor with God. 31 Now listen: You will conceive and give birth to a son, and you will name him Jesus. 32 He will be great and will be called the Son of the Most High,and the Lord God will give him the throne of his father David. 33 He will reign over the house of Jacob forever, and his kingdom will have no end." 34 Mary asked the angel, "How can this be, since I have not had sexual relations with a man?" 35 The angel replied to her, "The Holy Spirit will come upon you, and the power of the Most High will overshadow you. Therefore, the holy one to be born will be called the Son of God. 36 And consider your relative Elizabeth—even she has conceived a son in her old age, and this is the sixth month for her who was called childless. 37 For nothing will be impossible with God." 36 "See, I am the Lord's servant," said Mary. "May it happen to me as you have said." Then the angel left her.

At Rise

To understand the setting, we must journey back a couple of millennia to a little town, roughly 60 miles north of Jerusalem, called Nazareth. This story set in motion something that would change the course of humanity and all creation as God's plan of redemption came to earth. This moment was so astronomical that we would begin to measure time around it. Everything that came before would be known as B.C. (Before Christ), and everything after would be known as A.D. (Anno Domini, in Latin means "the year of our Lord").

What's more, the story of Jesus begins the New Testament, additional inspired writings that would be added to the Hebrew Scriptures (what we now call the Old Testament). Roughly 400 years had passed between the writing of the last book of the Old Testament (chronologically probably Ezra or Nehemiah) and the events of the New Testament. The Old Testament tells the story of God's creation, the fall of man, the law, the history of Israel, and the prophecies Israel received (including those telling of the coming promised one).

The scene is set for the arrival of the long-awaited one prophesied. The Savior that the Jewish people would have been hungering for, especially in this time of Roman occupation and rulership from the puppet king Herod, though His plan of redemption was so much more significant. This unwed girl, Mary, would carry that promise, but the road before her would be challenging in this society. The journey of faith for her and her betrothed is extraordinary. Soon, this couple would find themselves in a new setting, the city of Bethlehem, between 60 to 90 miles from Nazareth, for a census. While this sounds like an untimely road trip, this census perfectly aligns and prepares the way for prophecy fulfillment.

"Bethlehem Ephrathah,
you are small among the clans of Judah;
one will come from you
to be ruler over Israel for me.
His origin is from antiquity
from ancient times"- Micah 5:2(CSB translation)

God's perfect handwriting is written all over this story. The birth of the Messiah paved the way for every other story in this book and many more, including testimonies today.

The Scene

Miracle.

The very definition of the word is surprising.

But my word for this moment is *astonishing*.

I may not know the reason why.

To call that day a surprise

Would minimize,

What I felt inside

As my heart began to fly.

Awe,

Wonder,

Amazement,

Delight,

As I saw your plan before my very eyes.

A mix of emotions.

A thrilling commotion,

Beyond my wildest imagination.

God's promise set into motion.

Not an illusion.

No!

The words spoken provide hope,

Redemption.

The announcement of God's plan of salvation.

It seemed like an ordinary day.
My mind miles away
Filled with a beautiful array
Of hopes,
Dreams.
Though these words seem so small,
Compared to your plan on display.

Your thoughts are higher,
Your plans are greater.
This moment had been prayed for,
It seems like for forever.
But never,
Did I imagine my thoughts from bride,
Would shift in a moment to thoughts of mother?

But on that ordinary day,
In that ordinary place,
This ordinary girl,
Would behold a heavenly face.

This warrior angel,
His presence filled the space.
Yet, amongst the strength,
I also saw beauty and grace.

He greeted me.
Called me *favored*.
The look on my face must have uncovered, emotions.
Perhaps I looked troubled.
Is this fear?

Is this joy?
My heart raced,
The beat doubled.

"Fear not",
He continued:
"I bring you good news,
You will conceive,
give birth..."
The perfection of heaven was about to meet earth.

And though I had questions...
I could not fully perceive,
How this virgin womb would somehow conceive,
But with God,
the impossible is possible,
So, I simply believed.

And so this ordinary girl,
In that ordinary place,
Experienced extraordinary grace.
The Messiah would soon know this mother's embrace.

And I knew in that moment that nothing else mattered,
Because no matter how hard,
No matter the pain,
Whether I am shunned,
Or whether there are eyes of shame,
Even when others doubt,
I will claim the promise.
Proclaim His name.

Remember the day the angel came.

So, on this silent, oh so holy night,
With a star of wonder,
Star of bright,
My heart is filled with the purest delight,
As my eyes behold You the light.
Light of the world,
That is who you are.
But as I look at you,
All I see is my miracle baby in the light of the star.

My sweet baby boy.
Never have I felt such joy.
My boy.
Though joy to the world,
I know you will be...
For now, I will savor this moment you're here just with me.
Peace.
Quiet.
Let me just sit here and breathe.

Who could imagine a king in this space?
Who would imagine this pouring of grace?
In this little town of Bethlehem,
Heaven meets Earth in a beautiful embrace.
And I, your mother, kiss your sweet baby face.
Embrace You,
My son,
In this place.

Where will you go with these tiny feet?

Will these tiny hands meet the people's needs in the street?

Will they know who you are when you speak?

Will your road be easy?

Will your road be hard?

Do you know your journey?

To begin to think of these things only makes this mother worry.

So, to this moment, I'll cling.

And while I wish I could provide a room fit for a king,

As I look in your eyes, my whole being can only sing.

My baby boy,

The newborn King.

Sleep in heavenly peace,

Sleep in heavenly peace.

The Story

The scene has been set. The planning is underway! A young man and a young woman have begun their plans for one of the most memorable days of their lives, their wedding. Mary, the leading lady of this story, was a young teenage girl, thought to be between the ages of 13 - 16. Her character analysis could include words such as humble, young, ordinary, willing, obedient, and faithful

For Mary, songs of bridal bliss and exclamations of congratulations filled the air. For young Jewish girls, this day was one they prepared for their whole lives. It would have been the time to start the festivities and prepare for her next chapter with Joseph, her groom-to-be. The celebration was underway in Nazareth as two ordinary families planned to unite an ordinary, young teenage girl and her betrothed, ordinary carpenter fiance.

The word betrothal is not common in today's vernacular. Engagement is the more familiar word today, but the two words are not synonymous. The word engagement does not hold the same weight as betrothal. Modern engagement begins a season of planning toward a wedding day, where two lives make an eventual covenant, committing themselves to each other for life. The word betrothal, in the first-century Jewish context, delineated an approximately one-year engagement, during which preparations for the couple's lives together would be made by the couple and their families. While not itself marriage, to be betrothed signified the beginning stage of a covenant relationship between bride and groom. Breaking an engagement today, though not simple by any means, might mean having some difficult conversations, returning a ring, and a couple going their separate ways. In Mary's time and culture, breaking a betrothal was far more complex because it was already legally binding. To break the Betrothal covenant would mean going through a legal divorce. Understanding the significance of betrothal is essential in understanding the magnitude of what happens next, not just for Mary but also for Joseph.

While Mary and Joseph and their families were preparing for their shared future, God's plan for the future of humanity would soon make His entrance on the scene. A plan foretold in prophecies for centuries. A plan longed for but was unexpected in how it occurred, especially with this young girl. This plan would offer hope to the world and simultaneously threaten Mary's plans. This teenage, betrothed, ordinary girl is about to receive news that will change her life and the trajectory of humanity for eternity.

Scripture does not indicate that something spectacular preceded the announcement to tip Mary off to what was in store for her. Yet unbeknownst to her, an angel appeared to a prophet named Zechariah months earlier, announcing that his barren wife, past the age of conception, would conceive. Their child would prepare the way for God's Messiah. That angel, Gabriel, would also appear to a virgin, Mary, announcing that she would conceive and bear the Messiah.

Stop and ponder the grace of these two miracle conceptions. Within months, an older barren woman and a young virgin girl conceived babies. That older woman was Mary's cousin. How gracious not only for these miracle babies to be cousins but for Elizabeth to provide a safe space and affirmation to this young girl, Mary, about to step into a beautiful but difficult journey, as the angel Gabriel comes to Mary and announces she has been chosen among women to be the mother of the promised Messiah. Read Luke 1:39-56 for this part of the story.

What did this announcement mean for Mary? Was there a thrill of hope and a rush of excitement? Did she look over her shoulder to see if another young girl was in the room? God's plan used an ordinary girl to take on an extraordinary role. While this story is beautiful and celebrated each year at Christmas with yard nativity scenes, cherished manger scenes decorating the house, and even young kids acting out the manger scene with a baby doll as Jesus, in reality, Mary's obedience would come with immense sacrifice and focus on God's plan rather than what her plans for her life would have been.

Imagine Mary's conversations: "Mom, Dad, I have amazing news ....I am pregnant, but don't worry, I'm still a virgin. The child is God's. I am carrying the Messiah." Would her parents be as willing as Mary to accept this extraordinary news, or would they think what the town gossips would be thinking? "Oh no, Mary, what have you done? There's no way you are chosen to be the Mother of the Messiah. You're just Mary." And if that wasn't enough, she also had to tell her betrothed, Joseph. Her plans for her life just a day ago now rest on whether or not those she loves believe the unbelievable. And that's just the family side, not to mention the rest of the town.

Mary was not the only one who faced potential shame. Her family would face that same shame. Her future security was suddenly not so secure. Joseph had the full right to break their engagement. Remember, this was not just giving a ring back; this would mean a legal divorce. A pregnancy outside of marriage could only mean a few things. 1. Joseph and Mary did not wait for their wedding day, which would cause shame on them and their families. 2. Mary committed adultery. 3. Something happened to Mary unwillingly 4. She was the mother of the promised one. For Mary, not only was public shame a possibility, but in an extreme case, there were legal rights to stone her to death. This part is not usually told during the Christmas pageant.

With all that was at stake, Mary stepped into this role. Eventually, Joseph knew that Mary was telling the truth as an angel also appeared to him in a dream, and he ultimately stepped out in faith, believed Mary, and remained betrothed. However, it does not mean that society believed. And so, at the end of this teenage girl's pregnancy, in perfect timing to fulfill prophecy, Mary and Joseph make the journey to Bethlehem for a census, placing them in the exact location prophesied that the Messiah would be born.

The census involved people journeying to the land of their direct ancestors, placed amongst Roman soldiers. And when Mary's time to give birth arrived, there was no room for them except for a stall for animals. So this girl, with her husband as her only help, would give birth to the King of kings in a dirty stall for animals. She would not have the medical accommodations of a hospital or the comfort of a warm room. She would not have had the experience of a midwife or the soothing words from her mother. It was just Mary and her carpenter husband. Imagine the intensity and questions as each contraction came. Is this supposed to happen? Is my baby okay? Am I okay? Is it supposed to feel like this? Would there be embarrassment as Joseph was the only one there to help her, yet the two had not known each other intimately yet?

But on that silent night, in that little town of Bethlehem, the savior of the world was born. He came in the most humble of ways. He came as a baby, fully God and fully man. He could have chosen to be born in a royal house with the best accommodations, but instead, He was born to an ordinary girl in a stable, humbly. This miraculous birth would change Mary's life forever and everything for humanity, as God's rescue plan of redemption physically came to earth as a baby.

The Backstory

As an actress, I've had the chance to play various characters. Each new role begins the adventure of character development and seeing the world through their eyes to tell the story in the most dynamic way possible. The rehearsal process is a time of discovery and transformation. Writing, rehearsing, and performing spoken word is an in-depth, precise process. The words are chosen carefully, edited, and adjusted until the rhythm and words collide perfectly.

So, the rehearsal process began for Mary's Monologue. I often take my walks and rehearse, drive in the car and rehearse, and walk around the house as my dog follows me, wondering what I am talking about while I rehearse. The goal is to capture the moment and tell the story.

Stepping into a role is a learning process. So, for Mary, the process included a variety of emotions. From the delight of engagement, the awe, wonder, and fear at the sight of an angel, and the overwhelming feelings of the calling at hand. Then, the moment of the performance came. As I looked down at my arms, shaped as if holding a baby, and imagined looking down at baby Jesus, tears flowed down my face. These were not acting tears. While I can act my way through to make it look like I am crying, I have never been able to fake tears. If I'm crying on stage, it's real. As I spoke the words rehearsed, I imagined looking at my savior's face not as a man but as a newborn baby dependent on His mother, and my heart was moved. The glitter and glitz of what we see at Christmas was stripped away as I imagined new motherhood through Mary's eyes, overwhelmed by the love of a mother and the love of our savior who humbly came as a baby.

The Scene Study

- Imagine the thoughts and feelings that might have gone through Mary's heart and mind when the angel announced that she was chosen to be the mother to the Messiah. Write what might be a journal entry from Mary's perspective.

- How do you see God's grace for Mary and the world in this story?

- Put yourself in the manger that night. Think through Mary and Joseph's eyes. What goes through your mind when you look at that baby boy for the first time?

- What takeaways from this story can inspire and motivate you in your story?

- Reflect. God uses ordinary people to do extraordinary things. What does this mean to you?

The Senses

The sound of Christmas music can be heard worldwide during the Christmas season. People sing songs that point to the Messiah, sometimes without fully understanding the meaning. Sounds of praise are sung, even if the musicians do not fully know the depth of meaning in the lyrics. Find a place, and sing praise to King Jesus, unashamed, full belt. Consider reflecting and singing some of your favorite Christmas songs about Jesus (Oh Holy Night, Silent Night, Oh Come Let Us Adore Him ...Mary Did You Know). Take time to embrace the words and proclaim them. Write a reflection on your time. What did you hear, what did you learn, how were you inspired?

Chapter II

The Religious

The Scripture
John 3:3 - 21 (CSB)

1 There was a man from the Pharisees named Nicodemus, a ruler of the Jews. 2 This man came to him at night and said, "Rabbi, we know that you are a teacher who has come from God, for no one could perform these signs you do unless God were with him." 3 Jesus replied, "Truly I tell you, unless someone is born again, he cannot see the kingdom of God." 4 "How can anyone be born when he is old?" Nicodemus asked him. "Can he enter his mother's womb a second time and be born?" 5 Jesus answered, "Truly I tell you, unless someone is born of water and the Spirit, he cannot enter the kingdom of

God. 6 Whatever is born of the flesh is flesh, and what-ever is born of the Spirit is spirit. 7 Do not be amazed that I told you that you must be born again. 8 The wind blows where it pleases, and you hear its sound, but you don't know where it comes from or where it is going. So it is with everyone born of the Spirit." 9 "How can these things be?" asked Nicodemus. 10 "Are you a teacher of Israel and don't know these things?" Jesus replied. 11 "Truly I tell you, we speak what we know and we testify to what we have seen, but you do not accept our testimony. 12 If I have told you about earthly things and you don't believe, how will you believe if I tell you about heavenly things? 13 No one has ascended into heaven except the one who descended from heaven —the Son of Man. 14 "Just as Moses lifted up the snake in the wilderness, so the Son of Man must be lifted up, 15 so that everyone who believes in him may have eternal life. 16 For God loved the world in this way: He gave his one and only Son, so that everyone who believes in him will not perish but have eternal life. 17 For God did not send his Son into the world to condemn the world, but to save the world through him. 18 Anyone who believes in him is not condemned, but anyone who does not believe is already condemned, because he has not believed in the name of the one and only Son of God. 19 This is the judgment: The light has come into the world, and people loved darkness rather than the light because their deeds were evil. 20 For everyone who does evil hates the light and avoids it, so that his deeds may not be exposed. 21 But anyone who lives by the truth comes to the light,

*so that his works may be shown to be accomplished by
God."*

At Rise

It was late at night when Nicodemus, the respected religious leader,
and Jesus, the radical teacher, had a life-altering meeting. The specific
timing would lend itself to a secret meeting at night with fewer eyes on
the street and less possibility of being seen. Given the hatred towards
Jesus from most religious leaders, the timing made sense. However,
Nicodemus still made a bold choice to speak face-to-face with Jesus.
He was seeking the truth, even if the truth would change his world
forever. The meeting was risky for him, holding the world as he knew
it on the line. So, with curiosity and questions, Nicodemus disregard-
ed the possible controversy and stepped into this meeting place. No
matter the time or place, whether in secret or public, Jesus is always
ready for a divine appointment.

The Scene

Was it curiosity?
Intrigue?
A glimmer of divine light?
What was it that brought me here in the middle of the night?

We called Him teacher, Rabbi.
Names of prominence.
But I sense,
Through what He's done,
That He is much more immense.
Many of my friends find in Him great offense.
They are always on the defense.
They think He misrepresents all we've studied and achieved.
Hence why I am here at night
To figure out what I believe.

In quiet,
In secret,
I came alone.
Did I sense Messiah in His tone?
I had to know.

In all my studies and education
I should know the description.
He is not what I imagined in my interpretation.
But I can't deny that He has left an impression.

In Him, the paradigm shifts.
Can my heart and my head align as I sift through the words I've read
And the words heard from His lips?

I've come this far.
I'm here,
It's time,
In front of me, He sits.

My first words of the conversation,
"We know".
Was I afraid to admit my questions?
Did I want to lump others into the conversation?
Was I worried about my reputation?

I continue,
"We know your teaching; it comes from God.
No one could do the things you do
The signs
The wonders
Unless God is with you".
Was this a question or a statement?
Or did I already believe it?
Evidence is what I was needing.
I am a teacher of the law.
The people look to me for leading.
So why are we the leaders struggling,
While others have a clear understanding.

He responded so simply,
"You must be born again".
What?
How?
I don't understand.
I can't comprehend.

Are you saying that me, a grown man,
Must enter my mother's womb again?

What He was saying could not happen physically.
Was I just supposed to let logic concede?
Or was my religiosity making it hard for me to see...
Hear what He was trying to say to me?
Was I Stopping only at curiosity?

Or was this an absurdity?
Who is this in front of me?
Is He crazy?
Or does He have authority?
Which, if so
He would have to be...
Messiah.
Could He be?

Is He the manifestation of the words I've read?
Or am I just trying to fit him into what I have created in my head?
Are we, the Pharisees relying on...
Studies, philosophies, our abilities?
As a Pharisee,
I've worked hard to be
Admired,
Revered,
A figurehead of society.
I must have strong evidence to accept the feeling I have inside of me.

Most other Pharisees are angered by what they have seen.
But for some reason, I continue to seek, listen, glean.

"How" formed the beginning of my following questions.
"How can someone be born again when they're old?
How can this be?"
"You are a teacher".
He knows me.

His words continue.
"You speak of what you know and have seen
But you do not accept our testimony.
I speak of things that are earthly.
But what happens when I speak of the heavenly?"

His message was clear.
It was less about me.
Less about works and religiosity
And more about this Son of God.
But Believe.?

I am a man of tradition.
You know this about me.
I am a Pharisee.
No one knows the words of the law better than me!

Believe?!
That is all you are asking of me!
Be born again.
Are you speaking of this physically or spiritually?
And yet He speaks with such simplicity.
Am I lost in works and religiosity,
Making it impossible to see clearly who's in front of me?
When it's based on my works and following the law,

That is easier for me.

I asked him to meet secretly in the night.
Was I afraid of being seen in His sight?
The others are out to prove He's wrong
And they are right.

Yet...
He came.
Through my hesitations, questions, exclamations,
He answered with no reservation.
There was no condemnation.
It's like He welcomed them.
As though He cared about the relationship
More than tradition.
It was more than just religion.

I am a learned man.
I don't change my mind flippantly.
I need to know what I need to do to achieve anything.
Everything.
And yet He spoke of love from God
A love that asks us to simply believe,
And live eternally,
Because God gave His son for us freely.
Could this be...
Is the son of man in front of me?

The Story

Nicodemus was a fascinating man. On paper, he would appear to be a first choice, popular pick for the role of head disciple for Jesus. His resume seemed perfect. So, who was Nicodemus, and what were his outstanding qualities? Nicodemus was not just a Pharisee, though that alone meant a lot. He was among the religious elite of chief priests and likely the Sanhedrin. Yes, those very same chief priests who constantly sought to plot against Jesus and eventually were at the center of the scheme when Jesus was crucified. All this is to say that Nicodemus had many layers, and each layer only adds to the risk involved in this story.

The fact is, Jesus' disciples were not the expected choice. Jesus' disciples were a motley crew of people from various social standings, backgrounds, political ideologies, career choices, and opinions. In today's society, Jesus' group of disciples, pre-meeting Him, would probably argue venously about their varying beliefs on social media. From fishermen to a tax collector to a zealot, just to name a few, Jesus' disciples were an unexpected group. What a beautiful picture of opposing groups coming together because they experience transformation as their lives find common ground in Jesus.

To understand Nicodemus and his possible dilemma, we must understand his social group. Who were these men? In Matthew 23, Jesus spends an entire chapter addressing the Pharisees. At first glance, it would appear that Jesus was praising the Pharisees. "Do whatever they tell you, observe it." However, Jesus goes on to say, "Don't do what they do because they do not practice what they preach." Ouch! So, these guys knew the law; they knew the words. Their head knowledge was immense. These were the guys with the answers and influence.

However, when it came to living by example, the Pharisees were all about themselves, being puffed up and burdening others. They placed a heavy emphasis on tradition for the sake of tradition.

If tradition is at the center, and being elevated above others is important, then Jesus' approach and message would not fly with the Pharisees. Jesus' message speaks of love and freedom in Him. The Pharisees puffed themselves up, holding tightly to the law, leaving little room for grace. The Pharisees clearly opposed Jesus. Time and time again, the Pharisees tried to trap Jesus, using various questions and tactics. They questioned him for healing on the Sabbath and were divided on the answer (John 9:13-38). They tried to trap him with a question about taxes (Matthew 22:15-22). They even used the extreme shaming of a woman caught in sin to trap and challenge Jesus (John 8:3 - 11) (more on this story later). This was the crew that Nicodemus was associated with, yet there is something about Nicodemus that does not fit the standard description. While most Pharisees asked questions to trap Jesus, Nicodemus asked questions to seek Jesus, to seek answers. While the Pharisees plot to trap Jesus, Nicodemus sought a moment to meet with Jesus. While the others use public space to try to catch Jesus, Nicodemus seeks a secret space to talk with Jesus. Nicodemus sought the truth, even if the truth was not popular, even if the truth rattled his traditions and understandings.

Imagine each step he took in the quiet of that night. What questions would have been swirling through his head? As a well-educated man, what verses from the Torah would be circling on repeat? Was he comparing words he had read with Jesus' teaching? He would know the law and prophecies. He would have all of the head knowledge you could imagine. As he sought truth, there would be a question of belief. Would he choose to believe or stay put in his formed beliefs?

Finally, the time came for Jesus and Nicodemus to be face to face. He must have recognized something different about Jesus. He stated how he must be from God. Was he analyzing his studies to the person sitting before him? Did he imagine the Messiah to look and act differently? Had he created an idea of what and who the Messiah should be? What would come of this midnight meeting?

We don't know whether Nicodemus believed at that exact moment! What we do know is that Jesus welcomed the conversation and the questions. Jesus' answer left Nicodemus wondering, "How can a person be born again?" Jesus would answer and share the message of love and salvation found in Him.

Nicodemus is found in scripture three times. The first time is this famous conversation. Within this conversation came the words of one of the most memorized verses: "For God loved the world in this way: He gave his one and only Son, so that everyone who believes in him will not perish but have eternal life." (John 3:16 CSB).

The second mention of Nicodemus in scripture consists of him questioning the Pharisees in a discussion about Jesus, pointing towards belief or the beginnings of belief. In John 7, the Pharisees gathered to discuss why Jesus was still not in custody. Nicodemus uses their very own law to question what they are doing "Nicodemus—the one who came to him previously and who was one of them—said to them, "Our law doesn't judge a man before it hears from him and knows what he's doing, does it?" (John 7:51 CSB). Nicodemus boldly stood up for Jesus among his group, who fiercely opposed Jesus.

The last mention of Nicodemus in scripture points to a decision of belief in Jesus as the Messiah. In John 19, Nicodemus is seen with

Joseph of Arimathea as they plead with the Roman Government to release Jesus' body to them. They then took His crucified body, anointed the body with oils, and placed Jesus' body in a tomb. This action was in direct opposition to what Nicodemus' friends would be doing at this exact moment—a group who would have been leading the crowd calling for his crucifixion. Nicodemus and Joseph's decision was one of extraordinary boldness—an outward expression of his belief.

We don't know the story of Nicodemus from this point on, but when you take all of the information together and analyze it—just like Nicodemus would have done—what do you see? Nicodemus, an intelligent, respected man, a man of excellent social standing, a curious man, was willing to risk everything to seek answers, to seek the truth. Nicodemus was unwilling to stay on the bandwagon if it took him in the wrong direction. He fought to find the truth and sought what to believe for himself.

It is safe to conclude that this moment with Jesus changed everything. The transformation may not have been instantaneous, but in his seeking, the seeds of truth had been planted. Perhaps he needed time to process. Perhaps he needed time to read the scriptures and seek answers. Nicodemus did not just let others dictate his worldview despite extreme circumstances and the risk of losing everything. On the line for Nicodemus was his position, respect, social standing, livelihood, and potentially his life, yet Nicodemus still sought Jesus. His questions point to connection. He wanted to know, no matter what.

Each person's moment of belief looks different. Some come to know Jesus as a child, others through trials, others through witnessing a miracle, others through processing and seeking.... It is essential to understand that no matter what, no matter where you are on the journey to believe, Jesus is not afraid of your questions. He is not afraid of knowing what is genuinely on your mind, what you might be struggling with. Nicodemus came to Jesus humble and honest. As he sought Jesus, Jesus met him. No questions asked. All that was left was to believe.

The Backstory

One of my favorite courses to teach is introductory public speaking. Why? Statistically speaking, this is one of the top phobias people have, sometimes even surpassing the fear of death. My goal as a public speaking teacher is to teach students that they have a voice and to provide them with the tools to use their voices best. One of my favorite assignments as a high school teacher was the end-of-the-year assignment for my junior public speaking learners entitled "Why you believe what you believe?" I did not want them to give a speech stating what they thought I wanted to hear. Instead, I hoped to cause learners to ponder, reflect, and verbalize the "why" to their beliefs. The assignment was not easy, but in the end, most learners said this was their favorite speech. What we believe affects every element of life, from decision-making to a moral compass to the why behind our purpose.

If I was going to ask my students to give this speech, I needed to share mine as well. So, if you were sitting in my classroom, you would have heard me say that the Bible has come to life for me so many times, and today, I will give you three moments when I feel God held me in His hands. Moments that His presence was undeniable. Are there more than three reasons why I believe? Absolutely YES! But in my five-minute speech, I could only give a few.

The refined version of this question would be, "Who do you believe Jesus to be?" This is the question Nicodemus faced. This is the question everyone faces. There is no denying that a man named Jesus existed and lived. For Nicodemus, he could not deny the power and authority he saw but had to wrestle with the outcome of the answer. Jesus, for him, was either Lord or Blasphemer. Today, many believe He existed as a prophet, teacher, or a good man... but they are missing the fact that He was and is Lord. The answer to who He is changes the trajectory of everything else in life now and life eternal.

The Scene Study

- Put yourself in the shoes of Nicodemus. What were the things that were making it hard for him to believe? What similar hurdles to belief in Jesus do you note today? Have you experienced hurdles to your belief?

- Do a side-by-side comparison. What was the difference between Nicodemus' seeking and the other Pharisees seeking? Compare their process, ideas, seeking, and the result. What do you notice about the rest of the Pharisees' approach to Jesus compared to Nicodemus?

- Thinking of your own story, how has Jesus met with you? How might He want to meet with you today? Whether He has met you as you read this book, or whether you have a story of a time Jesus used a sermon, a worship song, a person, or a circumstance to speak to you...Write your story.

- Considering the above questions, what are some questions you have regarding Jesus? What might it look like to bring these questions to Jesus? What excites you about that idea? What fears do you have about doing so?

The Senses

Find a quiet moment of the day and meet one-on-one with Jesus! Be intentional about the space. My favorite quiet moment is at about 5:30 in the morning, with a cup of coffee as the sun rises. The house is silent, the dog is still sleepy, and Jesus and I can meet. Come to Him and seek a relational moment. Pray, not just a prayer of wants, but talk to Him. Leave room for Him to respond through His word. If you are still trying to figure out where to begin, read the book of John (reading may take days or weeks; the timeline is up to you). The Book of John is an eyewitness account of Jesus' ministry. As you read, stop and process (like Nicodemus). Stop and pray. Journal the details, small and large, that stick out to you. I'll leave you a few pages of space to process in the back of the book. Draw, write, and respond to what you learn about Jesus as you seek Him.

Chapter III

The Outcast

The Scripture

John 4:1 - 30 (CSB)

1 When Jesus learned that the Pharisees had heard he was making and baptizing more disciples than John 2 (though Jesus himself was not baptizing, but his disciples were), 3 he left Judea and went again to Galilee. 4 He had to travel through Samaria; 5 so he came to a town of Samaria called Sychar near the property that Jacob had given his son Joseph. 6 Jacob's well was there, and Jesus, worn out from his journey, sat down at the well. It was about noon. 7 A woman of Samaria came to draw water. "Give me a drink," Jesus said to her, 8 because his disciples had gone into town to buy food. 9 "How is it that you, a Jew, ask for a drink from me, a Samaritan woman?" she asked him. For Jews do not associate with Samaritans. 10 Jesus answered, "If you knew the gift of God, and who is saying to you, 'Give me a drink,' you would ask him, and he would give you living water." 11 "Sir," said the woman, "you don't even have a bucket, and the well is deep. So where do you get this 'living water'? 12 You aren't greater than our father Jacob, are you? He gave us the well and drank from it himself, as did his sons and livestock." 13 Jesus said, "Everyone who drinks from this water will get thirsty again. 14 But whoever drinks from the water that I will give him will never get thirsty again. In fact, the water I will give him will become a well of water springing up in him for eternal life." 15 "Sir," the woman said to him, "give me this water so that I won't get thirsty and come here to draw water." 16 "Go call your husband," he told her, "and come back here." 17 "I don't have a husband," she answered. "You have correctly said, 'I don't have a husband,'" Jesus said. 18 "For you've had five husbands, and the man you now have is not your husband. What you have said is true." 19 "Sir," the woman replied, "I see that you are a prophet. 20 Our ancestors worshiped on this mountain, but you Jews say that the place to worship is in Jerusalem." 21 Jesus told her, "Believe me, woman, an hour is coming when you will worship the Father neither on this mountain nor in Jerusalem. 22 You Samaritans worship what you do not know. We worship what we do know, because salvation is from the Jews. 23 But an hour is coming, and is now here, when the true worshipers will worship the Father in Spirit and in truth. Yes, the Father wants such people to worship him. 24 God is spirit, and those who worship him must worship in Spirit and in truth." 25 The woman said to him, "I know that the Messiah is coming" (who is called Christ). "When he comes, he will explain everything to us." 26 Jesus told her, "I, the one speaking to you, am he." 27 Just then his disciples arrived, and they were amazed that he was talking with a woman. Yet no one said, "What do you want?" or "Why are you talking with her?" 28 Then the woman left her water jar, went into town, and told the people, 29 "Come, see a man who told me everything I ever did. Could this be the Messiah?" 30 They left the town and made their way to him. (John 4:1-30, CSB)

At Rise

The scene began with so much excitement. Ministry was happening! Baptisms were taking place. The number of followers of Jesus was growing. It looked like a scene of revival, though to the Pharisees, the scene caused alarm. On that note of revival, Jesus and His disciples began a journey to Galilee. Instead of taking the expected long route around Samaria, Jesus broke cultural, social, personal, and spiritual barriers by taking the direct route through Samaria.

The Samaritans and the Jewish people—though, to be clear, the Samaritans were of Israelite descent as well—had a long-standing family rift dating back to the Old Testament. This rift was so strong that it was common for the Jewish people to avoid Samaria altogether when traveling. It did not matter if the journey would be longer; what mattered was avoiding Samaria. Remember, we are not talking about taking the scenic route home on a road trip in a car, with the air conditioning going, as Spotify plays your road trip playlist. To avoid Samaria and take the long route meant extra miles by foot, or maybe donkey if you're lucky. This choice of avoidance was extremely intentional.

Jesus walked straight through, passionately pursuing the people the others would have pridefully avoided. So, as the curtain rises on the scene, it is the heat of the day—noon. This is an important note as we approach the well.

The Scene

This road,
I it know well.
Every day, I take my path to the well.
Day by day.
Journeying at the time in the day when no other makes their way.
It's an isolated pathway.
It's better that way.

Yes,
I've heard all the names.
I've seen the looks of shame.
Every time.
Every line.
Every raised eye.
And all I wanted to do was get by.
Avoid the eyes.
Shy away from it all.
Forget the names I've been called.
Yes, I've heard them all.

No one cared to get to know me.
They think they know the whole story.
Filling in their blanks to my story,
Without knowing me fully.
Never mind that we each have a story.
Pages of our history.
Words that create lines
And begin to define us,
As line by line, the words intertwine.
Over time,
Shame had become the word that defined every one of my lines.

So alone, I walked.
It was easier that way.
Until the day all that changed.
Until I saw him face to face.
I can't explain it,
In a moment...
I saw grace.

In a place where I used to feel disgraced,
Something new was about to take place.

Something was different as I approached the well.
Why is this Jewish man in this place?
Does He not know I'm a disgrace?
An outcast.
Let alone the issue of race.
I'm a Samaritan.
And to add to that, a Samaritan woman.
Why was He even willing to share this space?

So I approached timidly.
Perhaps if I move quickly,
He won't notice me.
But then suddenly,
Unexpectedly,
He spoke.
Why is He asking for water from me?
Does He know who I am?
"How do you ask this of me, a Samaritan woman?"

But to my amazement,
To my surprise,
I did not see judgment in his eyes.

He continued,
He went on to say,
"If you knew who talked to you today
You'd say,
Give me living water.

You'd never thirst another day.
And it would be given to you today."

So of course I say,
"Give me this water
So I'll never be thirsty.
So alone at this well, you will never again see me."
Could I dare to allow hope in me?
Allow my walls down for some stranger to see.
Obviously, this was too good to be.

As He continued, all good things must come to an end.
With the following words, I knew I could not pretend.
He said,
"Go grab your husband."

Dread.
It filled my cheeks, making them red.
Once He hears about me,
This offer will flee.
I will remain thirsty.

"I have no husband."
But He knew there was more to the story.
He knew without any words from me.
How could He know this?
I don't understand.
As He said,
"And the man you live with is not your husband."

He went on to say all the things I had done.
Who is this man?

Is He a prophet that has come?

Yet, for some reason, the beat began to change.

He knew all my sins,

Yet this was different.

He did not rub them in

Or use them against me.

It's as though He wanted more for me.

Like this moment was supposed to be.

Could it be,

He came here to this well just for me?

"I've heard of Messiah"

He said,

"I AM HE."

No!

Could it be?

But at that moment, I knew.

My eyes were beholding the King.

My heart began to sing.

But why would He, the Messiah, talk to me?

Yet, looking in his eyes, the questions began to flee.

Something began to take over me.

A peace,

A calm,

A joy I'd never felt.

Let me savor this moment.

Forever let me feel what I felt.

It's like nothing I can explain.

His eyes made me forget the shame.

So I ran!

Not to hide.

I ran to the city,

Leaving my water jar.

Leaving everything with me behind.

You see in His eyes

I felt the fear subside.

As I cried,

"Come and see a man who told me everything I ever did!

Could this be the Messiah?"

And the people, they came.

That day will forever be the beginning of my new story.

The Messiah, Jesus,

Changed my life for me.

Made a new creation out of me.

Set me free.

So, as you look at me,

What you see is a woman who represents

A life changed by Him.

Impossible became possible.

Not because of me,

But because of Him.

The Story

The name of the story's leading lady is unknown; she is simply called the Samaritan Woman at the Well. Possible words for her character description could be outcast, alone, broken, hard life, guarded, rejected, bold... The beauty of this story is in the details. In one moment with Jesus, everything changes; the walls come tumbling down as instantaneous transformation occurs.

Scripture is clear that she came to gather water at Jacob's well at noon. At first glance, this seems like a minor detail, but in reality, it is a significant detail that uncovers many layers of her story. During this time, there were no faucets or modern amenities to provide drinking water, which was/is not a luxury but a necessity for life. To fulfill the need for water, someone from the family would have to gather water from the well and carry it back. Imagine the size of the jug, the weight of the water, and the walk to and from. Back in the day, this chore was often performed by the women of the town. They would gather together and journey to get the water early in the morning. There was safety in numbers and coolness in timing. Put yourself there. As most girl gatherings go, I imagine these trips included lots of chatting and perhaps even a little gossip.

So why was the Samaritan Woman at the well going to get water at noon, once it was hot and no one else was around? Perhaps she was not invited to the water party or wanted to avoid the social situation altogether. Was she the topic of conversation and gossip? Then again, perhaps she was not the topic but feared the possibility of becoming one. But on this day, she would not be alone. She would find not just drinking water but water for the soul. A divine appointment was waiting for her at the well.

Barriers were about to be broken as Jesus and his disciples traveled from Judea to Galilee, breaking the cultural norm by taking the direct route through Samaria. Jesus was about to compassionately crush cultural and personal barriers in one conversation. Beautiful!

The disciples went on an errand to buy food. Jesus sat by the well-wearied from travels as a broken woman with a past approached to complete her daily water chore. Any hope she might have had of being alone was instantly shattered. Not only was she not alone, but she was in the presence of a Jewish man who asked her to give Him water. Her immediate response is all too common when brokenness becomes the main descriptive word for the story. She not only disqualified herself once, she disqualified herself three times in a matter of a few sentences. "How is it that you a Jewish man?" disqualification 1 - you are Jewish and a man. Disqualification 2, and I am Samaritan, and I am a woman, disqualification 3. Culturally, the races would not interact, let alone those of the opposite sex. Basically, I am not qualified; move on and let me go on with my lonely chore of gathering water. But Jesus was not afraid of her response. He continued His pursuit. Again, Jesus is asking questions during the conversation. Questions open up conversation rather than condemnation or commandments.

The conversation continues. Jesus offered the woman living water. The idea of gathering water is the beginning of this whole story. The woman missed the water party, revealing her isolation, perhaps even labeling her an outcast in the community. Jesus offered "Living Water." Perhaps she simply thought, well, that sounds nice; water that lasts forever would make this social avoidance a thing of the past. Of course, she would welcome the idea of not carrying water in the heat of the day. How often do we look at something Jesus says and think so small or immediate? While the physical quenching of water is wonderful, even a necessity for life, Jesus was talking about so much more. He was talking about spiritual renewal, transformation, and a new life in Him.

Perhaps the walls were beginning to break as the woman said, 'Give me this water." Jesus continued with the following statement, "Go bring your husband." A quick snap back. Walls up. That subject seemed off-limits. "I Have no husband." Just as the walls went back up, Jesus was about to tear them all the way down. Jesus would go on to tell her everything she'd ever done. The revelation of His knowledge that she has had five husbands and the man she was living with was not her husband.

The reveal above is a lot and could mean so many things. A woman's role at this time was to be a wife and mother. It would be easy to assume that she must have been a discontent woman; maybe she was after something each time, but those are assumptions. What about these other possibilities? Was she barren, and therefore, the men asked for divorce? A possibility of the times. Did she make the mistake of adultery? Did a husband die? Was it a combination of the above? To be barren back then was to be looked down upon, even giving cause for the man to divorce his wife. Adultery was and is a sin. The death of a husband would be out of her control. Scripture does not give the details, but what we know from the story is that Jesus knew the details. This man she just met would go on to tell her everything she had ever done.

It is easy to imagine her as a conversation topic; good news travels fast. Surely, she had heard the rumor mill, yet at this moment, as Jesus tells her everything she has ever done, she reacts interestingly. Though truthful, Jesus responds with grace. Was there a glimmer of hope in her eye? Did she already know the answer as she said, "I know the Messiah is coming...When He comes He will explain everything to us." Jesus then answers what was probably already twirling in her mind. "I, the one speaking to you, am He."

The magnitude of this moment is monumental. This moment is the first instance in the book of John where Jesus reveals Himself to be the Messiah! Sit with that for a second. He did not reveal himself to Caesar, the king, the chief priest, or Nicodemus (the previous chapter in John's account). The exact revelation, the word-for-word confirmation that Jesus was the Messiah, was given to a Samaritan Woman with a broken past for the first time. As much as we may try to hide our past and stay isolated, not to expose ourselves, Jesus knows our past! He knows the detailed version of every moment. Just like Adam and Eve tried to hide themselves in the garden with no success, we cannot hide from Jesus.

Psalm 139 states,

> *Lord, you have searched me and known me.You know when I sit down and when I stand up; you understand my thoughts from far away.You observe my travels and my rest; you are aware of all my ways. Before a word is on my tongue, you know all about it, Lord. You have encircled me; you have placed your hand on me. This wondrous knowledge is beyond me.It is lofty; I am unable to reach it.*

> *Where can I go to escape your Spirit? Where can I flee from your presence? If I go up to heaven, you are there;*

if I make my bed in Sheol, you are there. If I fly on the wings of the dawn and settle down on the western horizon, even there your hand will lead me; your right hand will hold on to me. (Psalm 139:1-10 CSB)

In His knowledge, He still chose to reveal "I am He." Beauty and grace are the words for this intentional meeting. No matter our story, Jesus can make us new, and this story reminds us of this as an unlikely woman in an unlikely place, at an unlikely meeting, was offered an unlikely gift that changed everything.

The result. The woman at the well would be the first recorded evangelist! She left her water and ran to the town to tell them about this moment with Jesus. "Come and see this man who told me everything I had ever done...Could this be Messiah?" She went boldly to the same town that already knew everything she had ever done but perhaps did not care to know the details, only caring about the narrative they had written. She boldly told her story, not for her glory, but for God's glory, and because she boldly went, many came to know Jesus! Lives were changed. One moment with Jesus can change everything, and the change keeps multiplying when we boldly go in His name. That day, as she sought physical water to sustain her, she found living water to transform her. Jesus' living water is an invitation to let Him sustain us, refresh us, cleanse us, and provide us with new life, and it is offered to each of us today.

The Backstory

Let me tell you about a time I shared my story with roughly 250 women from my home church at a women's retreat. There was a mix of feelings, from familiarity to feeling uncomfortably new. I would share my story in spoken word format with parts I had only shared with my inner few. Would people understand or think I was weird? Would my story make sense or fall flat? How vulnerable should I be?

As the writing began, I prayerfully penned my story. Jesus and I worked through broken, triumphant, and miraculous parts. The writing was my time with Jesus, and little did I know healing was taking place. Perhaps what I felt, though our stories were different, was similar to the woman at the well—gentleness, love, compassion, and eventually restoration from my savior.

Throughout, disqualifying thoughts tried to take over. Shame was trying to take center stage, but Jesus is always intentional. Jesus is greater. Jesus is stronger (1 John 4:4). Just as these accusatory, shameful thoughts began, one of my mentors walked by the table I was working at. Instead of listening to the sermon in church that day, I was writing at a church cafe table. She came up, we chatted, and she prayed over me. She encouraged me to share this current struggle when I share my story. I love how God provides! I reluctantly added the current battle and found that in doing so, in being authentic, not just to share past moments of my story but to include the here and now, a prayer declaring truth over lies surrounded each rehearsal. The beginning part, the first part memorized, the part practiced the most because it was at the beginning, was all about the current offense from the enemy. Each time I rehearsed, due to the structure of the piece, a prayerful defense using truth was declared.

In the end, I told my story for God's glory. What did I find? People could identify because it was real. Using my story, even the hard parts, gave me added healing by proclaiming the victory found in Jesus.

The Woman at the Well is one of my favorite stories. Did you know this woman with a sordid past holds the record for the longest recorded conversation with Jesus? Her story gives each of us hope. Her story is an inspiring reminder to tell our stories for God's glory.

The Scene Study

- What words have you used to disqualify yourself from a moment, a step out in faith, or a relationship with Jesus?

- How do we see Jesus break cultural, personal, and spiritual barriers?

- Jesus' offer of living water went far beyond the physical need. He met this woman where she was and offered her a new life. How has Jesus met you personally and offered something beyond what you could comprehend?

- How does this woman's full story from before Jesus to after her encounter with Jesus encourage you? Be detailed.

The Senses

- We each have a story. Each story comes with varying moments, from joyous moments to triumphs, to trials, to brokenness. Every story is different. Right now, spend time on your story. Find a quiet place and write your story down. Below, you will find a simple starting point.

  - Before Jesus I was.......Then Jesus......Now I am.....

  - Think of milestone faith moments, prayers answered, transformation, triumphant moments, joyous moments, miracles....

  - As you write your story, spend time with Jesus; let this be an intentional time with him.

- If you still need to invite Jesus into your life, still do the exercise. Simply write from a place of what you have learned about Him. Who is he? What have you seen Him do in other people's lives, now or in the Bible?

Chapter IV

The Paralyzed

The Scripture

Luke 5:17-26 (CSB)

17 On one of those days while he was teaching, Pharisees and teachers of the law were sitting there who had come from every village of Galilee and Judea, and also from Jerusalem. And the Lord's power to heal was in him. 18 Just then some men came, carrying on a stretcher a man who was paralyzed. They tried to bring him in and set him down before him. 19 Since they could not find a way to bring him in because of the crowd, they went up on the roof and lowered him on the stretcher through the roof tiles into the middle of the crowd before Jesus. 20 Seeing their faith, he said, "Friend, your sins are

*forgiven." 21 Then the scribes and the Pharisees began
to think to themselves, "Who is this man who speaks
blasphemies? Who can forgive sins but God alone?"
22 But perceiving their thoughts, Jesus replied to them,
"Why are you thinking this in your hearts? 23 Which
is easier: to say, 'Your sins are forgiven,' or to say, 'Get up
and walk'? 24 But so that you may know that the Son of
Man has authority on earth to forgive sins"—he told the
paralyzed man, "I tell you: Get up, take your stretcher,
and go home." 25 Immediately he got up before them,
picked up what he had been lying on, and went home
glorifying God. 26 Then everyone was astounded, and
they were giving glory to God. And they were filled with
awe and said, "We have seen incredible things today."*

At Rise

We know from the parallel passage in Mark (see Mark 2:1-12) that
this story takes place in Capernaum, a town on the coast of the Sea of
Galilee that held significance as a trading center, Roman military post,
and customs station. It was situated on a well-used road leading from
places such as Egypt in the south, Damascus in the North, and Tyre
in the west. This meant that not only did the town host visitors from
many diverse cultures, but it was also home to both Jews and Gentiles
(non-Jewish persons).

On this day, people traveled from near and far. The passage does not point to any specific festival or event, which would seemingly lend itself to the fact that Jesus' popularity was growing, and people wanted to see Him. The streets were crowded, and the house was filled with people trying to get a glance at the teacher Jesus. There was standing room only, and barely at that.

The Scene

Paralyzed.
Hopeless.
Helpless.
This is how I was identified.
So you can only imagine how this day came as a surprise.

Picture with me this incredible scene.
People crowded together just to be seen.
To see this man.
Glean from His words.
Maybe be healed.
Even become clean.

I had no expectations that day.
But all I can say is,
Thank God for the friends He gave.
Today, they fought for me to have a new day.

Pushing through a crowd.

Carrying me.

Because all I could do was just be there and lay.

That was how I lived every day.

But they were determined to find a way.

They did not care what people might say.

Even if I'd lost hope,

Today, they would not let hope slip away.

Now you have to imagine the reality.

What it took in actuality.

Through a sea of people,

Each pushing their way to see.

And then there's me,

A man on a mat with four people carrying me through the streets.

People were everywhere.

And honestly, It's not easy to just lay there,

Take in all the stares.

Not to mention the whispers and glares.

Try to imagine how humiliating this would be.

But they found a way.

So, suddenly, a spark of hope began to flame.

Do I dare hope to be lifted from this cursed shame?

Would today be the day I no longer lay here lame?

But the crowd only intensified.

Crowded side by side.

My friends tried,

But soon realized,

We couldn't get inside.
Even when it seemed easier to let hope die,
They were going to find a way inside.

I can't believe what they decided to do.
The plan to get inside was to climb to the roof
Then lower me through.
The task may sound easy,
But think about it honestly.
Four people climbing while carrying a grown man, me.
Not to mention the looks of the people who could see,
And as if that's not enough, remember there is still a roof separating
Him from me.
But even that was not a reason for them to give up and leave.
They dug through the roof with no worry about liability.
I can only hope you have friends like me.
Friends who fight for you fiercely,
Even when it seems like hope is an impossibility.

So they began to lower me.
They bore the weight of me
With the added pull of gravity,
Ignoring any pain for them there might be.
Careful not to drop me,
They placed me down carefully.
Now, I could finally see.
I was face to face with the man in whom my friends believed.
His name was Jesus,
And we were the center of the crowded scene.

The people surrounding me were not just anybody.

They were leaders and Pharisees.

Would they welcome or reject me?

But clearly, this Jesus was all that mattered, really.

His words are words I will never forget,

"Your sins are forgiven."

My friend's belief

Made an impact.

But these were not quite the words I thought to expect.

My sins are forgiven?

It was so calm and direct.

But did he neglect to see the paralysis?

Should I even interject,

Or be grateful and just accept?

Yet somehow, I felt in my heart that what He was giving me

Was bigger than any miracle I could even begin to expect?

Even if I still lay here,

This gift I could not reject.

But before I could make a sound or a cry,

Immediately, the words began to fly.

The Pharisees cried,

Blasphemy!

Questioned His authority.

Only God can forgive sins!

Though their words were harsh, it's also the reality.

So, the thought came to me,

If He has the power to forgive me,

Does that make Him deity?

Without hesitation

Jesus asked them questions.
It's like He had precise knowledge of their thoughts beyond simple intuition.
He asked which is easier to heal this man,
Or to say your sins are forgiven.
He did not use it as ammunition.
He calmly gave an invitation to ponder and think about the conclusion.

So when He looked at me,
Said to me,
"Take your mat; get up and walk."
I got up.
Took my mat.
And Walked!
With all eyes on me,
The impossible was achieved.
My feet moved in front of me.
I took steps like it was a daily activity.

But you see,
While the physical healing was what we went there to seek,
With friends who dared to intercede.
The miracle of forgiveness,
I can't possibly express fully...
The impact that means.

So look for the miracle that is more than you asked
More than you can conceive
Even the miracle of friends who are there to stand with you in faith

And believe when it's hard for you to believe

The Story

Have you ever desperately wanted something? What was it? Perhaps a relationship, healing, a dream deferred, that job.....This desired moment is something that will seemingly change everything. What happens when there is a time of waiting? What happens when an answer is given, but it is not quite the answer expected?

Welcome to this man's story. A situation desperate for healing, with little hope for that to occur. Paralyzed, dependent on others, hopeless, and helpless could be words used in this man's character description. Scripture does not say how long he was paralyzed, but it does state that he was a grown man carried on a mat. In addition, many in Jewish society at this time believed that crippling ailments such as blindness or lameness could be a result of sin. (Read John 9:2-41 to see this thought process displayed).

Enter on the scene four people who are the epitome of friendship. When hope seemed lost, four determined friends carried their friend to the one in whom hope could be found. The journey of the friends and this paralyzed man may appear easy and seamless, at least when we are simply reading the word on a page, but in reality, this task would have taken a strong belief and determination.

Imagine the scene. The friends and man on the mat finally found their way through the crowd, arriving at the house where Jesus was. Upon arrival, they realize it's too crowded and cannot get inside. What next? Is it time to give up and say, "Well, we almost got you to Jesus, but it was too hard. Sorry." Luckily for this man, that was not the case. It was just an opportunity to solve a problem. Can you imagine everyone looking around for a great idea? Was the paralyzed man hopeful or embarrassed by the fuss of his friends? Then somebody speaks up with an idea. " How about the roof?" Instead of laughing at a seemingly ridiculous idea, the friends move forward.

Okay, pause and ponder the gravity of their solution. Yes, spoiler alert, the man received his miracle, but this middle detail is incredible. These friends stopped at nothing to introduce this man to Jesus. They quite literally climbed to the top of a roof with a friend whose only way up was to be carried. They were not going to miss Jesus that day. They pushed through no matter what it took. Talk about true friends. The task described would be physically demanding and possibly dangerous, not to mention the soon-to-be vandalism of a roof. Time for more ideas. "What if we lower him down?" Have you ever carefully lowered a grown man through a roof, slowly placing that man in the perfect position for healing? Incredible! Plus, the hole to lower the friend did not magically appear. The friends would have to create it. Imagine the looks from the people inside, specifically the religious leaders, as the hole appeared above them. Would they be welcomed or rebuked? Cheered or judged?

These friends teach the importance of carrying and supporting each other in times of weakness. This story shows the dynamic life change that can occur when we boldly bring others to Jesus, no matter what it takes! It is worth the hardship, the pain, and breaking down walls (or roofs) when encountering Jesus awaits on the other side.

Once lowered through the roof, now inside the house, the paralyzed man was finally face-to-face with the man everyone was trying to see. His eyes met the eyes of Jesus for the first time. Incredible, but Jesus' eyes were not the only eyes in the room. The man was the center of attention for the Jewish religious leaders of his day, those who likely blamed his disability on his sin; not an easy crowd. Would he feel complex emotions of anticipation, fear of judgment, not wanting to be the center of attention, and perhaps even a bit of hope?

It does not take long for the first miracle—yes, first, as in more than one to take place. Jesus speaks forgiveness over this man's sins. Now, if you are the man, perhaps there was a thought of, well, that's not exactly the words I expected, but okay, sure. In our modern minds, we might even think that he would have been disappointed, but re-member, physical healing would not have made him right with God, which is ultimate healing. It can be easy to miss the less visible healing, even if it is the more incredible healing. So, though unexpected, this man would have known the weight of this miracle. Jesus was effectively proclaiming this man clean and forgiven among the religious leaders who most likely would have called him a sinner (which we all are), but perhaps even cursed due to sin. Jesus revealed His authority, which was/is greater than that of religious leaders. This was huge. Jesus came to rescue us from our sin, everyone in the crowd then, everyone now. Jesus is revealing that He is the one and only way, eliminating the need for the priest to intercede on behalf of the people, now providing direct access to the one with authority. Himself!

The Pharisees were not happy. At every corner, as Jesus revealed His authority, the Pharisees remained blind and or unwilling to accept

Jesus for who He was revealing Himself to be. So, the drama continued to build. Jesus began to ask questions, displaying his knowledge of their thoughts. He could have just condemned the religious leaders, told them off, and said, "Who do you think I am? Open your eyes." But that's not Jesus. He asks questions, leaving room for reflection and conversation.

> *22 But perceiving their thoughts, Jesus replied to them, "Why are you thinking this in your hearts? 23 Which is easier: to say, 'Your sins are forgiven,' or to say, 'Get up and walk'? 24 But so that you may know that the Son of Man has authority on earth to forgive sins"—he told the paralyzed man, "I tell you: Get up, take your stretcher, and go home."- Luke 5: 22 - 24 (CSB)*

Again, Jesus directly revealed His authority by using a name that connects Him to Daniel's prophecy in the Old Testament, "Son of Man" (see Daniel 7). The prophecy in Daniel describes the one with this name as one given all authority and sovereign power. Jesus was making a bold declaration to all who were listening and willing to hear.

Jesus continued with the man. He goes for miracle number two and tells the man to get up and walk. The man has a choice now. Does he believe and step out, or stay with what he knows and remain on the mat? It is easy to stay in a comfort zone, even if that same comfort zone is what we long to escape. Logically, the simple words get up and walk would not seem like a cure for this man. It's too simple. If he tried and failed, it would be in front of a large, judgemental crowd. Sometimes, it is easier to stay in what we know, even if what we know is what makes us miserable, sick, or complacent. It can be easier to hold onto bitterness instead of letting it go and letting God heal, moving into joy and relational healing. We can get into a comfort zone of sin, even trying to justify our actions, knowing it's wrong. Stepping out of a lifestyle of sin seems scary, even if we know it is the best way. We can get comfortable in a location, a job, or something that might even be good, knowing we feel called elsewhere. It sometimes takes a step of faith out of the comfortable good and into God's best. Fill in the blank: life is full of opportunities to step out of our comfort zone, but we must take the first step.

This room has multiple reactions. There were the religious leaders who only saw what they wanted to see. They were comfortable in their pride. They had been waiting for the one before them, but they chose to stay instead of step. There were the four friends who believed so fiercely that they took hard steps of faith because of the one they were stepping towards. Then, there was the man carried to Jesus. Two miracles occurred. The first would not be the expected miracle, but ultimately the greatest one. The second miracle took him stepping out in faith, which he could do because he was listening to the faithful one.

The Backstory

Heartache defined the season. I had misplaced my hope and lost sight of my purpose amid heartbreak. I needed a breakthrough. At the time,

I was an incredible school's Director of Fine Arts. We were practicing for an upcoming performance, including staff, students, and guest performers. When we announced this performance, I challenged myself in a new way. For this night, I thought, why not play the piano? The thing is, I don't play the piano. I have always wanted to learn, so why not place a performance on the line to push myself to learn how to play? The kids heard me practice the same song and broken melody as my fingers learned how to work in this new way.

During the final rehearsal, the performance day, my fingers suddenly stopped working correctly. With eyes on me and voices waiting for me, everything began to crumble. Any ounce of confidence was gone. Shaken, I got up from the piano bench, went to my friend and fellow director, and said, "I'm not playing. You play, I'll sing, and the show will be fine. No one will know." The problem was I had let the moment be known to give myself real accountability. With a gentle nudge, he said something along these lines, "It's not about perfection. You have to play to show the kids you did it. You conquered the fear. Failure doesn't even matter. All that matters is that you get up and try."

The night went on. I paced when everyone was onstage. I walked quietly to a side of the theatre to watch the kids perform and pray. Simultaneous to my nerves and prayers were prayers and support from friends and family. They had recognized the fear on my face and went into action. It was time. I had to decide whether to get up and walk to the piano or not. And so I took one step of faith at a time. Faith in me? Not at all! I walked to the piano, sat down with the band surrounding, nerves rattling, emotions rising, not sure of the outcome, and placed my fingers on the piano and began to play. My heart is racing just writing this! Miraculously, the song happened, and just like that, it was over, and the joy began to take the place of fear, doubt, and even other feelings of heartache that had taken residence in my season of life.

Jesus is so intentional, so it makes sense that a performance would be used for me, a performer, to begin stepping into a new season. A beautiful restoration of my heart was beginning. That night happened because of faithful friends and family who helped carry me. The steps to the piano, the immediate pushing past fear, were used to help me step from the past into newness. Fear or no fear, success or failure, Jesus had me. With the gentle nudge of a friend and prayers carrying me, I knew I could not give the kids a message that fear is bigger than possible failure or bigger than God. Fear was not going to have the last word. But I had to get up and walk.

The Scene Study

- Put yourself on the mat? What are your feelings before this miracle? What are your thoughts as your friends make this decision? Do you fight them on it? How do you feel as you journey the crowded streets, carried on a mat?

- What character qualities do you notice from the friends in this chapter? If you have friends like them, describe them here. Thank God for them. Perhaps even thank them for their friendship.

- What would your feelings be as the first miracle, "forgiveness of sin," is stated? It is not the expected response, so what do you feel?

- Imagine what it would be like to believe in that moment, get up and walk. Write a reflection from the man's point of view. What do you imagine he did first? (Blank pages are added at the back of the book if you need more space to respond.)

- Do you find yourself in the role of the four friends, the person on the mat, or the religious leaders? Write a reflection and response. Why? Are there steps of faith you feel you need to take?

The Senses

Take some time to think of a friend who has impacted your life. Write down how they have impacted you. From there, spend intentional time with that friend. This could be a coffee together, a phone call, or even a letter written to them. Share how they have impacted your life and what you learned in this chapter that made you think of them.

Chapter V

The Unclean

The Scripture

Matthew 8:1-4 (CSB)

1 When he came down from the mountain, large crowds followed him. 2 Right away a man with leprosy came up and knelt before him, saying, "Lord, if you are willing, you can make me clean." 3 Jesus reached out his hand and touched the man. "I am willing," he said. "Be clean!" Immediately he was cleansed of his leprosy. 4 Then Jesus said to him, "See that you don't tell anyone. But go, show yourself to the priest and offer the gift Moses commanded, as a testimony to them."

At Rise

The smell of sickness was in the air. The intensity of fear enveloped the space. Leprosy had entered. Leviticus 13 -14 describes the customs, processes, and practices Israel was to take surrounding skin diseases. Diagnosing a skin condition included examination, quarantine, and repeating that process until satisfied through the eyes of the priests. All this occurs with the constant question of whether or not a person would be considered clean or unclean in the end. Leprosy was a diagnosis that would lead to the identification of "Unclean."—a status that, unless healed, would create separation from society and a permanent declaration of being unworthy to reenter society and reconnect with God through the temple system of the first century.

This was the context that brought this man to the road that Jesus was on all those years ago. On an ordinary road, on what would appear to be an ordinary day, an extraordinary event was about to take place.

The Scene

Unclean

The symptoms, unsalvageable,
The prognosis undeniable.
Unclean became my label.
The disease incurable.
Impossible to change.
Once identified, the outcome – unavoidable.
The full meaning of the word...
Unbearable.

Pain.
Misery.
Yes, pain Physically,
But the loneliness,
It drained me mentally.
Basically, I was consumed wholly by this identity.
The word Simply,
Leprosy.

The prescription,
Isolation.
I was forced away from human relations.
A life lived in desolation.
Not to mention,
Stripped of family.
No hope for my situation.
No more touch from another.
No eyes of care.
A safe distance between us.
Even that was more than most could bear.
Mouths covered so as not to breathe in the same air.

So I lived day to day,
Away.
With hardly the energy left to pray,
Wondering if God would even hear the words I had to say.
Or would He too step away?

Then there's my family.
Imagine with me,
Touch from my family would never again be,
As I watched them step away from me.
Afraid they would catch the disease.
Yet I could see they, like me,
Longed for one more touch before I had to leave.
This was a wish.
Only a dream.
No kiss.
No hug.
No running embrace.
No time in the field as we play and race.
No gentle touch from my wife as she touches my face.
No longer free to live in the same place.
Safety was space.

People don't often speak of such things.
Some subjects simply cause too much of a sting.
My reality was devastating.
So, the change now in me, in simple words, is amazing.

So why was this day different from them all?
You see, I had heard of a man.
Though that word now seems so small.

He was more like a Savior for all.
Not just religious.
Not just here for the rich.
He cares for the poor.
He cares for the sick.

So, I made the journey.
With my voice warning others I was there.
Unclean!
I took one step and then another.
Unclean!
Ignoring the stares.
Unclean!
With each step, I could feel the glares.

The people stepped back.
They, too, shouted unclean.
But He remained,
Looked at me.
For the first time in so long,
I felt seen.

The crowd tried to get further away.
Angered by my presence that day.
But He stepped closer.
Not away.
One step, then another,
He headed straight to me
Until we were face to face.
He was breathing the same air as me.
Yet in Him, fear was not what my eyes would see.

I saw eyes that saw me for me.
Not just my disease.

So, I dared to ask for healing!
I had to try!
What more could I be losing?
But what happened next was nothing short of amazing.
Before He answered, "I will,"
Before the healing came.
He did something extraordinary.
I will never forget it.
After years of agony...
I was so lonely.
He compassionately,
Reached out His hand,
And He touched me.
Who was this man in front of me?

The healing came.
The words proclaimed.
But that touch,
That was personal.
It declared a change in my name.

No longer Unclean,
The new word, Redeemed.
Divinely embraced.
Covered in grace.
No longer a disgrace.
Now, because of Him
I can face tomorrow.

Because of Him,
I have joy instead of sorrow!
Because of Him,
I have a new life instead of just waiting for death.
Because of Him,
I can breathe a new breath.

That touch,
That detail,
That part of the story,
It's a detail that seems so tiny in theory.
But in reality,
It's a detail of great enormity.
His simple touch,
It reminded me of my humanity.
That healing touch,
Filled the parts left empty.
I will never forget His detailed care for me.
The miracle within the miracle.
Compassion for my whole story.

The Story

The person entering the scene was not a long-awaited hero or a villain, though perhaps the fear surrounding his condition created a villainous persona. His life, in this condition, would have been painful, both emotionally and physically. Possible words to describe this character could be broken, sick, hopeless, cursed, sinner, outcast, and the final word declared when in the presence of others, "unclean." The diagnosis was leprosy—the prognosis, isolation, and separation. No cure! At least there was no cure at the time. As this skin disease spreads, it eventually deforms the body and limbs. Disfiguration and nerve damage and, in some cases, loss of limbs are possible results.

As if the physical ramifications were not enough, perhaps the worst part was the social and emotional pain accompanying this diagnosis. Life now would equal separation from loved ones and friends. To have this disease meant unavoidable isolation, a life sentence of six feet apart, in reality, probably even more. One day, you are with your family; the next day, you are living amongst the living dead, hoping for healing, but in reality, waiting to die. Human touch was eliminated. To touch someone considered unclean would, in turn, would make you unclean as well until proven clean, whether you caught the disease or not. So once diagnosed, no Touch, no hope.

Scripture does not say how long this man had suffered from leprosy, but let's imagine a probable possibility. It's a typical day full of work, chores, and maybe some family time playing with the kids. As this man prepares for the day, he notices a slight skin discoloration. It's probably nothing, right? But what if it's not nothing? You don't want to raise undue concern, but then there is your family; you also don't want to put them in harm's way. He's read the law, knows the possibilities, and understands the protocol. Questions overwhelm each thought. The instant mix of hope and fear sets in. Hope that it is nothing, fear that it is something. He is trying hard not to think of the worst possibility. He would eventually go through the Levitical instructions on skin. In case it is contagious, there would be a fear of touching your family and, again, a hope that it is nothing. "Let's just be safe through the process." The news would then come back. The worst is now a reality. Amongst all spoken, he only hears two words, "leprosy" and "unclean."

His life is changed forever.

No warning, no one last hug. He must leave his family immediately. As he walks away from his loved ones, their eyes meet. A mix of fear and love is expressed in his wife's eyes. He sees eyes of confusion in his kids. He holds onto those faces as long as he can. It's the closest he gets to embracing them. There is no hope to return to his home. Hopeless is his new destiny. While we do not know his backstory, this would explain a probable scenario for his life. This was the effect of leprosy.

The amount of time he spent living with leprosy is unknown, but what was known was his situation was hopeless. Enter Jesus, the living hope! How had he heard of Jesus? What had he heard about Jesus that gave him the courage for the journey? Did he endure stares, glares, and turned heads as he passed people on the road? Did he hide his sores beneath his garments to hide his condition, hide himself? Did people hold their breath in his presence or step back as he walked past? How long did he walk, declaring his given identity "Unclean" as was the command in Leviticus 13:45? Did others notice him and make the declaration for him? Did he try to hide who he was as he made the journey? Somehow, the man must have heard of Jesus because he boldly walked into His presence. We know other people were around, but this man was willing to risk it all for this one moment with Jesus.

Now, it is easy to look only at the miracle at the end of the story (Spoiler alert: the man does receive healing!) However, simply passing to the miracle means missing a small but massive detail. Listen to this!

The order of events matters. Before Jesus declared healing on the man, He did something unthinkable, powerful, and incredibly intentional. Jesus touched him. Jesus lived out the sermon on the mount, which He Just taught. He showed mercy. He helped this needy man; He showed love to a seemingly unlovable man. He was there for the poor in spirit. He exemplified His preaching.

Imagine the impact of this extremely compassionate touch. Remember, since his diagnosis, human touch was no longer a part of this man's life. Now add the pain of the fear in the eyes of everyone he met. Starved for human connection would have been his reality. Knowing the personalities of some of Jesus' followers, I doubt that they remained patiently quiet as a man with leprosy approached. So, as others would most likely step back in fear, Jesus stepped forward with compassion, face to face with the man declared "unclean." Jesus met this man where he was in this unique moment. He satisfied the starvation of the soul and touched this man with leprosy *before* He declared healing over his physical disease. In the eyes of the religious temple system, Jesus made himself unclean with this touch. But Jesus somehow passes on his fullness of body to the man, rather than the man passing his uncleanness onto Jesus. Jesus has no fear of this man. This simple act of reaching out and touching him showed great compassion and sovereignty combined - compassion for the man and sovereignty over the situation.

The fact is that touch was not a requirement for healing. In other miracles, Jesus healed entirely from a different place. Words alone could heal a person, not even in Jesus' presence. Just continue reading Matthew 8, the next chapter of scripture where the next miracle occurred outside of the sick person's presence. This story is also the next chapter of this book!

Jesus can heal in whatever way he chooses. Jesus spoke words, and the seas obeyed. Jesus commanded demons to flee with just words. Jesus even raised his friend Lazarus from the dead with words. Touch was not essential for Jesus to heal, yet, in this encounter, the detail of touch met this man in a very specific way. Jesus is personal! Jesus healed what doctors could not. Jesus cleansed what priests could not pray away. Jesus leaned into someone who everyone else feared. Jesus touched the man and *then* spoke His words of healing. These little details make an incredible impact on how we read this story.

This story shows both relationship and power. It's almost like there are two miracles: the emotional miracle and the physical miracle. In one moment, this man went from unclean to clean. His life changed in just one moment with Jesus!

The Backstory

2020! The year that brought the world to a halt, bringing words such as quarantine, isolation, and pandemic to the front of conversations. Phrases such as "Six feet apart" became the new normal. There was fear of both the known and unknown. How long would this last? Is it safe to go out? How do I get covid? How will I know if I have it? What happens next? Everything looked different. It was during the COVID lockdown, with more time on my hands, that this book began to be written, though I didn't know it then. As I read Bible stories and various books, I would reflect on the people I was reading about by writing spoken word poems about them. I used the countless free hours to read, reflect, and write. It felt like I was getting to know these Bible characters in a new and more profound way. I wanted to write from their perspective, to step into their shoes, and as I did, my eyes began to open.

As I read this story, I saw the similarities of fear, isolation, and quarantine existing globally. At that moment, though not entirely, I could imagine what it looked like to have people stay far away. We were living it. I remember visiting the grocery store within the first week of lockdown. People stayed far from each other, covered completely, afraid to get this illness that was stopping the world in its tracks. There was so much unknown at that time. Still not knowing how to respond, still with so many questions, I came home from that trip and quickly took a shower. I also remember finally hugging people again for the first time, a simple act so easily taken for granted, but not this time. There was physical relief and joy in the first hugs. When I read this story, though it does not compare thoroughly, I saw this man's story differently, with just a glimmer of understanding.

The Scene Study

- Write a reflection from the perspective of both miracles. What would Jesus' touch and healing have meant to you if this was your story?

- Now that you are physically healed, what would your response be?

- What does knowing that Jesus is both powerful and compassionate mean to you?

- How has Jesus met with you intentionally? If you are unsure, that's ok. Look at how he might meet you in small and large ways. Each detail matters.

The Senses

Stop and look around you! Who is hopeless, helpless, or lonely? Who is living amongst the dead or in a desperate situation? Who at your place of work, school, or church is lonely? Perhaps it is even you at this moment. Write a prayer for that person. Pray intentionally and compassionately, knowing that the prayer is powerful not because of your words but because of who you are praying to. Stop, think, reflect? How can you show this person intentional compassion? Perhaps it is a visit to a nursing home, a warm smile, asking someone how they are doing, or forgoing your usual seat at church to sit next to someone you have noticed is alone. How can we be the hands and feet of Jesus?

Chapter VI

The Authority

The Scripture
Matthew 8:5-13 (CSB)

5 When he entered Capernaum, a centurion came to him, pleading with him, 6 "Lord, my servant is lying at home paralyzed, in terrible agony." 7 He said to him, "Am I to come and heal him?" 8 "Lord," the centurion replied, "I am not worthy to have you come under my roof. But just say the word, and my servant will be healed. 9 For I too am a man under authority, having soldiers under my command. I say to this one, 'Go,' and he goes; and to another, 'Come,' and he comes; and to my servant, 'Do this!' and he does it." 10 Hearing this, Jesus was amazed and said to those following him, "Truly I

tell you, I have not found anyone in Israel with so great
a faith.11 I tell you that many will come from east and
west to share the banquet with Abraham, Isaac, and
Jacob in the kingdom of heaven.12 But the sons of the
kingdom will be thrown into the outer darkness where
there will be weeping and gnashing of teeth." 13 Then
Jesus told the centurion, "Go. As you have believed, let it
be done for you." And his servant was healed that very
moment.

At Rise

At this time in history, Israel was under the rulership of Rome. Roman soldiers working for the Roman government possessed governing authority over most of the Mediterranean, subjecting the people of those lands to their authority. A centurion would have been a high-ranking Roman soldier with at least 80 soldiers under his command.

Several parallel passages in Luke 7 point to the probability that this centurion was almost certainly based in Capernaum, a city blessed often with the physical presence of Jesus. Luke's story reveals that this particular centurion was unique, " because he loves our nation and has built us a synagogue"(Luke 7:5 CSB). This was not the typical relationship between the Jewish people and the Roman authorities. It is clear that this centurion was different, showing characteristics of humility, kindness, justice—and the people of Capernaum were grateful.

Capernaum, a fishing village off the Sea of Galilee (at the intersection of several important trade routes), was also home to a Roman military base. Matthew (the author of earlier scripture) seemed to live there (see Matthew 9:9-13), and it was also the home of the disciples Simon (Peter), Andrew, James, and John.

This just begins to paint the picture of the activity on the streets of Capernaum, setting the stage for a certain centurion to have a potential front-row seat to all Jesus did there. All the while, his faith—was building. Initially, he was just a man doing his job, but eventually, this man found faith.

The Scene

Strength.
Bravery.
Dignity.
The pillar of authority.
Perhaps some even fear me.
These are some words you might use to define me.
But I'd imagine,
You'd imagine,
There's no fear in me.

Just look at him.
No one could touch a Roman centurion.

In some ways, you'd be right.
I'm trained to win the fight.
My voice commands go left or right.
People look to me both day and night.
I decide what is right.

And I would bet that all you see in me is strength,
No humility.
You may even agree that humility is weak.
At least, that's what many think.
To be honest,
Until now,
I would have agreed.
But today, all that changed for me.
Perhaps now, I see
Strength in humility.

Let me ask you a question.
Maybe then you'll see through the lens with my resolution.
Have you ever cared for someone but did not know what to do?
And usually, you are the strong one.
People come to you.
But this issue,
It's beyond you.
There's nothing you can do.

So you watch them suffer.
No cure discovered.

And me, the one considered stronger than most others...
I can't do anything.
Only wait like any other.

But in my role, there was this one.
This man is often in Capernaum.
That's my post as a Roman Centurion.
Some believed He held truth.
Others questioned everything He would do.
His popularity had begun.
He was the topic of many discussions.
Some thought He was their promised one.
In others, He found rejection.
It was an interesting observation.

Then there's the stories of impossible things He would do.
Could they be true?
Yes, centurions have questions too.
We also have limitations.
I can't heal a man.
But for some reason,
After what I've seen and heard,
I think He can.

So I decide to approach and see.
Something in me believed.
But what will He think?
Will He speak to me?
Acknowledge me?
Does He know me?
This isn't like me-

To worry about what one man thinks.

But as I approach,
Get closer,
I see.
He exudes equal parts humility and authority.
How can that be?
I speak.
"Lord, my servant is paralyzed,
Lying in agony."

He begins a conversation.
"Am I to come heal him"
Was it a statement,
Or a question?

This man is not ordinary.
He is extraordinary.
I sense,
Somehow,
That I am in the presence of some kind of Royalty.
I call Him Lord.
A word I use rarely,
"Lord, I am unworthy.
Not worthy to have you under my roof.
But, like me, you have authority.
If you speak the words,
I believe,
My servant will be free from this disease."

I was not prepared for the words that came next.

He said He'd found no greater faith.
The effect of those words left me perplexed.

I am a centurion.
Many would call me the enemy.
But seeing Him face to face,
The only answer that makes sense in the presence of that kind of grace,
Is unwavering faith.

And right there, in that moment,
Healing occurred.
The space between didn't matter,
Only the power of His words.
Because of this one moment with this one man,
I am a forever-changed Roman Centurion.

The Story

In this story, two authorities collide in one powerful encounter. One authority was evident with just a glance of the eye, but in reality, his authority was limited. The other authority appeared ordinary at first sight. Not rich, no outer warrior garments announcing His power. Yet, at this moment, the centurion, the one with power by the world's standards, recognized his limited authority in this seemingly ordinary man's presence. He must have been observant, watching and listening to the events surrounding this Jesus of Nazareth. He was willing to humble himself to ask this seemingly poor Jewish teacher to help him heal, not his family member, not his friend, not his boss, but his servant.

The book of Matthew speaks often of Jesus' authority. In Chapter 7 of Matthew, Jesus gives the famous sermon on the Mount message, which ends with an observation that Jesus "he was teaching them like one who had authority, and not like their scribes" (Mt 7:29 CSB). This was a bold statement placing Him above the religious leaders. In Matthew 9, Jesus heals the paralyzed man and forgives his sins, something only God can do, which would ultimately reveal the deity of Jesus if anyone was willing to see and hear. In Matthew 10, Jesus gives the disciples authority to drive out impure spirits and heal. You can't give something you don't have. Matthew 28 holds the beautiful and powerful last words of Jesus before ascending into Heaven after His resurrection. Amongst His final words, Jesus states that "all authority has been given to him" (Matthew 28:18). Jesus' authority is incredibly evident. Yet, many who should have easily recognized him pridefully rejected Him. However, in this encounter where characteristically pride would be expected, it was laid aside as the Centurion humbly recognized his limited authority that paled in comparison. He found his faith in the one who was/is faithful and declared Jesus "Lord," a term he would expect to hear for himself.

So, what brought this Roman Centurion to this decision of faith? Let's look at what he may have observed. As an authority and leader, detailed observation would be essential to successfully enforcing the law and keeping the peace. Here are a few events he may have observed while on the job. In Matthew 4:12 -17, Jesus leaves Nazareth, His hometown, and makes Capernaum His new home.

Mark 1 is full of amazing accounts in Capernaum. Mark 1:16 - 20 depicts the moment that four fishermen from Capernaum decided to follow Jesus. These four fishermen are Simon, Andrew, James, and John. Luke 5:1 -11 adds detail to this story by describing the most miraculous catch of fish. Talk about some good news to spread through the town, "Did you hear about the fish? The net was so full it was ready to burst at the seems."

Luke 4:31-44 recounts Jesus teaching in the Capernaum Synagogue—a synagogue apparently built by this very centurion as a gift to the Jewish people of the town—driving out an impure spirit in a man. In Mark 2:1-12, Jesus healed a paralyzed man in Capernaum.

Why does all of this matter? This encounter with Jesus would seem very out of character for a centurion. His position was respected, a position of leadership. But here, this man lowered himself, even proclaiming that he was not worthy of Jesus entering his house. He called Jesus "Lord" when he would expect a grand title of respect from the people for himself. He believed in the power of Jesus so much that he was even willing to say that only Jesus' words would heal His servant.

When you break down the story, it is no wonder Jesus declared amazement over this man's faith. He did not make his request in the privacy of his home. He did not force Jesus to come to him. He did not wait for Jesus to pass him casually on the streets. This centurion sought Jesus out urgently. Scripture says, "When he entered Capernaum, a centurion came to him, pleading with him. " (Matthew 8:5 CSB).

The faith of this centurion is fascinating. This man did not grow up going to the synagogue, sitting in school, learning about the scriptures and prophecies. Perhaps he knew the stories from what he heard and observed as a soldier among the Jewish people, but this was not a family tradition or a cultural norm for him. He would not have grown up in anticipation of a Messiah, but now he is a leader amongst a very religious people group with strange traditions different from his people.

This story challenges us not to miss the details around us daily—observe what Jesus is doing in our midst even today. And with this challenge, we also receive a cautionary tale. Jesus did not praise the religious leaders for their faith. Many of those considered the most religious questioned Jesus. It would be the religious leaders who eventually plotted the capture and ultimate execution of Jesus. These were the same ones who should have known who Jesus was and understood his authority because they were anticipating the coming of the Messiah. Yet this pagan Roman Soldier observed and put his faith in Jesus in a way that amazed the Messiah.

May we have eyes that see Jesus all around us, observing every detail, and the courage to passionately and humbly seek Him out in faith, declaring Him Lord, just like this Roman centurion.

The Backstory

I wanted to understand the people written about in scripture so that each dramatic interpretation would accurately depict the inner workings of each character or at least a plausible idea of what the encounter was like through their eyes. Each session involved writing, searching, and discovery, and in the process, these stories were coming to life in new, powerful ways. At one point, I found myself singing the lyrics to the old worship song "In the Secret" (now I'm dating myself). The theme of that song is to know God more. The more I dug deep, the more this happened because while the stories of the people are incredible, diving deeper into the character of Jesus through their stories was awe-inspiring.

The dynamics for this chapter seemed easy. At first glance, Jesus and the centurion would seemingly be the perfect protagonists and antagonist counterparts, but this centurion was complex, leaving me with a question. *How?* How is it that this man, a high-ranking non-Jewish soldier, would have this kind of faith? Jesus even affirms his faith. What, when, and how did he come to possess "so great a faith" in Jesus? (See verse 10)

So, I began researching and found a detail that changed my entire perspective on who this centurion was. Excited, I had to share what I discovered with my husband. Bless his heart for being married to a storyteller. It involves lots of patient listening, with all of the dramatics included.

"Jon, did you know that Jesus lived in Capernaum? It was kind of like His ministry headquarters." Jon was so sweet to listen and chat all through this process.

The thing is, I had read the scriptures about Jesus' time in Capernaum before and never thought much about the location. But this time, I was seeking an answer to a question. Scripture is full of details that

God can use to illuminate passages in ways that connect afresh with our hearts, minds, and lives. It was and is a reminder never to stop seeking the details found in the stories of the Bible—to be open-handed in learning and growing. God has new things to reveal to each of us every day.

The Scene Study

- Write from the Roman Centurions Perspective. Imagine hearing and or seeing the stories listed above as law enforcement. What would your report of the events be? How would that impact a bold decision of faith? Be detailed in your response.

- The Centurion sought Jesus, while many of the religious leaders rejected Jesus. What can we learn from a side-by-side comparison of the centurion and the religious leaders? What differed in their responses to Jesus?

- Define humility as you see it in this story.

- Reflect on the intentionality of Jesus. Think about the story of the man with leprosy and this story of the Centurion with faith—side-by-side stories in scripture. Name the differences and similarities. How do you see Jesus' intentionality as you compare each story?

The Senses

Over the next week, observe and journal. How do you see Jesus during this time of observation? Look for him in everything. Consider the beauty of creation and observe the artistry of God the Creator (John 1:1-3). Think of light in the darkness and remember that Jesus is the light of the world, and where there is light, darkness is defeated (John 1:4-5). Observe how He may use people to bless you through (a smile, a hug, a word spoken, a kind gesture, an encouragement....). How does He reveal Himself through His word? Read one of the gospels (Matthew, Mark, Luke, or John) and observe Him through His life lived on earth. Observe, reflect, and write. Try to write at least one observation a day, but feel free to write more.

Chapter VII

The Sinner

The Scripture

John 8:1 -11 (CSB)

8 Jesus returned to the Mount of Olives, 2 but early the next morning he was back again at the Temple. A crowd soon gathered, and he sat down and taught them. 3 As he was speaking, the teachers of religious law and the Pharisees brought a woman who had been caught in the act of adultery. They put her in front of the crowd. 4 "Teacher," they said to Jesus, "this woman was caught in the act of adultery. 5 The law of Moses says to stone her. What do you say?" 6 They were trying to trap him into saying something they could use against him, but Jesus stooped down and wrote in the dust with his finger. 7

*They kept demanding an answer, so he stood up again
and said, "All right, but let the one who has never sinned
throw the first stone!" 8 Then he stooped down again
and wrote in the dust. 9 When the accusers heard this,
they slipped away one by one, beginning with the oldest,
until only Jesus was left in the middle of the crowd with
the woman. 10 Then Jesus stood up again and said to
the woman, "Where are your accusers? Didn't even one
of them condemn you?" 11 "No, Lord," she said. And
Jesus said, "Neither do I. Go and sin no more."*

At Rise

A crowd had gathered at the temple to hear a message from this intriguing rabbi, Jesus. Somehow, in the middle of His teaching, a nameless woman, caught in the act of adultery, was humiliatingly brought out and placed in front of the crowd. A spectacle of shame was on display. Honestly imagine the gravity of the situation for one minute. Imagine being at church with a crowd of people. There is anticipation in the air to hear a message from a teacher rapidly gaining popularity. Then suddenly, you are dragged up onto the stage, in the middle of the sermon, your deepest sin displayed for everyone to see and judge.

As if the public shaming wasn't enough, simultaneously, the Pharisees were plotting against Jesus. They found the moment they'd been waiting for in this woman. How did this opportunity come to them? Did they happen upon the sinful act? Was this a setup? Whatever the case, none of the answers seem like an upstanding start to their day. Were they excited to find these two in sin so they could trap Jesus? Their relentless approach is a cautionary tale, never to find excitement in another's sin. Instead, we should help lead others to the redemption Jesus offers. The extreme punishment in the Jewish law for her was death. (Deuteronomy 22:22).

It is important to remember that this land was now ruled by the Roman government, adding a new layer to the scene and the trap set for Jesus. Roman law would prohibit the Jewish people from enforcing capital punishment. (See John 18:31) So Jesus was seemingly in a no-win situation. To condemn her would follow the Law of Moses and appease the Pharisees, but would break the Roman law. To let her free would go against the Law of Moses but remain in line with the Roman law. The Pharisees had seemingly set the perfect trap at this church service turned courtroom drama.

The Scene

Chaos surrounds me.
Shame sinking deeply.
Taken instantly from intimacy to this humiliating scene.
Shamed publicly.

Surely, this is the end of me.

Emotionally,

Spiritually,

Maybe even physically.

My depravity dragged out to the street.

My sin exposed for all to see.

Naked.

Surrounded.

Uncovered.

Ashamed.

Called by my sin

Not by my name.

Yes, I know I'm to blame.

You don't need to remind me of my shame.

If only time could rewind.

Regret fills my mind.

The Images of what I did climb.

Thoughts and emotions Intertwine.

I know right from wrong,

But, the right choice was declined.

I assigned my worth to mankind,

I let temptation win.

Chose sin.

I knew what was right, but let wrong in.

No one will save me.

Not even the one who took part with me –

Taking part of me.

Where is he?

Did he leave?

Did he go free?

Obviously, my worth is just pennies.

So alone, I face my destiny.

They've declared my identity.

I am the woman caught in adultery.

They asked the teacher what He thought should be done with me.

What judgment would He place on me?

The leaders who brought me seem bloodthirsty.

They are ready to place the ultimate penalty.

They have the right to stone me.

It's the law.

Are they just trying to make an example of me?

Will no one have mercy?!

Hope is lost.

I know I traded my life for a clear line that I crossed.

I can't look up.

I'm too afraid.

Besides, what would I say?

I've sinned; I know that I must pay.

I can't deny why they brought me here today.

Then I see the teacher through the corner of my eye.

Would He cast the first stone?

What?

Why?

Why is He now by my side?

In His shadow, I felt like for a second I could hide.

He spoke to the crowd.

Just a simple phrase.

"He who is without sin cast the first stone."

I can't bear to see His gaze.

Then He knelt.

I watched his finger glide.

Guide each grain of sand.

His hand a brushstroke in the sand.

Each stroke moved with command.

What is this persuasion I hear singing?

It can't be!

Am I imagining things.

I hear the sound of stones clinging.

1,2,3,

One by one, my condemners are leaving.

4,5,6,7

I don't understand.

What is happening?

What did He write in the sand with his hand?

What had they seen?

There is a drastic change in the scene.

Hope.

Fear.

Relief.

Grief.

All at once, these emotions combined.

When I look up, what will I find?

But I know it is time.

Afraid to move.

Afraid to speak.

I hear him speak.

"Woman".

Where are they? Has no one condemned you?"

The words.

I can barely speak.

"No one, sir."

"Neither do I. Go. Sin no more."

With these words, tears filled my eyes.

I could only fall to my knees and cry.

I once was lost, but now I see.

Mercy.

Mercy beyond what I could conceive has been given to me.

Others, including me, only saw my life as piled debris.

Broken.

Shattered.

Unworthy.

But His eyes tell a new story.

It's like He sees me for me,

Not just my sin.

It's as though He is looking deep within.

While others looked away,

He looks in.

As His eyes continue to reach mine,

A thought comes to my mind.

He assigned life when death was on the line.

Who is this teacher?

In Him, somehow, I feel I can start again.

It's like I am a New Creation.

So today, I am leaving behind the name "Adulterous Woman."
I am making a new declaration,
As I exclaim:
"Redeemed is my new name!"
This man has restored and covered my shame.

The Story

This story is seemingly small, only 11 verses long, yet profoundly large in its impact. Perhaps you noticed a small caveat to these verses in your Bible. And you may be asking why. It seems this story was not found in the original manuscript written by John, causing debate among theologians over the years. There are several theories concerning how this story may have been added to Scripture. This discussion could take the rest of this chapter. One simple possibility is that this story was circulating. The passing down of stories aligns culturally with the tradition of oral storytelling. This story could be just that. The fact of the matter is that this story aligns with the gospel message. It shows the Pharisees' path to plot to kill Jesus, which would eventually happen. It displays Jesus' amazing grace. Therefore, there is much we can glean from this text.

So, let's peel back the beautiful details in this sordid story. A woman quite literally caught in the act of adultery. I'll say it again. She was not followed to a restaurant where pictures were taken. Her phone was not hacked, revealing scandalous texts. She was caught in the literal act of adultery and caught in the most vulnerable state possible. She was used as bait to trap Jesus.

There is so much to consider. First off, it takes two to commit adultery, so where was the other person? Did these men want to trap Jesus so badly that nothing else mattered, no one else mattered? Was her life just collateral damage in the Pharisees' plight to trap Jesus? What was her story? With questions about the situation come questions about the accusers. These men were leaders. They knew the law. They would have known the prophecies best. So, shouldn't the Pharisees, the religious leaders, be the first ones to identify Jesus as the long-awaited Messiah? Shouldn't they see prophecy fulfilled within this man they are trying to trap? Was it pride that kept their eyes blind? Whatever it was, they were now taking their hatred for Jesus to a new level, as a Jewish festival turned into a courtroom drama with the death penalty on the line.

Now, let's not ignore the truth. There was/is no question about this woman's guilt. The facts cannot be sugar-coated. She was in the wrong. No one, including Jesus, is denying that. And in that day and age, the extreme judgment could be death by stoning. Words to describe this woman's character analysis could include sinner, adulterer, shamed, vulnerable, and lost. We don't know her backstory, leaving room for a million possible descriptive words to fill in the depth and details of her character, but this is all that is known.

Enter Jesus on the scene. Before an entire crowd, Jesus calmly shows both love and authority. He does not shy away from the matter of sin. He approached the topic with a question, "He who is without sin cast the first stone?" Best mic drop ever! He left no room for anyone to begin an argument and compare sin to sin. No one had the right to say they had never sinned, well, except for Jesus. Self-righteousness has no room to exist in the presence of Jesus. He was clear and concise, leaving no room for error. "He who is WITHOUT sin…" Yet at the same time, at this exact moment, stood the only one without sin. Jesus, himself, was/is perfect, sinless. Yet, instead of casting a stone, He drew or wrote in the sand. Oh, how I wish I could see the outcome of what His fingers gliding in the sand made. Whatever it was, the stones dropped, and one by one, the accusers left. Was it His words? Was it what He created in the sand? Was it a combination of the two that caused stones to drop instead of being thrown?

He then asks her a question. "Woman, has no one condemned you?"

She answers, "No one."

Jesus responds, "Neither do I. Go and sin no more."

A response soaked in grace. He did not turn to her and cast stones of judgment, figuratively or literally, even though He fell into the sinless category. He did not just walk away once the work was completed and the drama died down. Instead, He asked a question. He was inviting her into a deeper moment. He is relational, not transactional. By asking, He has opened the moment up for a conversation. Imagine how she would have felt as the situation went from death to life.

We don't know where that woman went after the day's events. One could speculate and hope that this moment with Jesus changed her life forever. It only takes one moment with Jesus to change everything, but it is still our choice to lean into Him. He pursues us with the greatest love but will never force His way into our hearts.

What we do know is that Jesus, the only one with the true credentials of perfection who could have condemned her, offered redemption instead. New life to replace the old life. Life vs death. This moment is a beautiful image of us ALL. This moment is for the seemingly most religious person, all the way down to the one who is sitting in prison because the consequence of their sin is condemning them to death. Jesus, fully God, fully man, did not condemn her in that moment but offered her salvation from death, forgiveness of sin, and a new start. Jesus didn't even condemn the ones who were quite literally there to bait Him. He simply makes a statement and begins to draw in the sand. The calm of Jesus is incredible.

Jesus is so constant. He came to "Seek and save the lost" (Luke 19:10). He is the good shepherd who would leave the ninety-nine for the one lost sheep (Luke 15:1- 7). Yet, at this moment, many had the opportunity to change. The woman, yes! That's obvious! But what about the Pharisees? What about those looking in on the situation? One moment with Jesus can change everything. It's our choice to accept Him and allow the change. There is life after what we consider our greatest sin; the opportunity is there to repent and live as a new creation in Christ. No matter how publicly humiliated or how much your private shame carried deep within may be, there is new life offered for all.

No one is too far gone from the grace of Jesus.

The Backstory

Shame! It's a powerful word that can evoke strong feelings. It is different than the word guilt. Guilt reveals the crossing of a boundary. Shame is that debilitating word that keeps us stuck. Stuck from moving on. Stuck in unforgiveness towards ourselves. Stuck feeling God can't use us. Stuck from accepting there is a better way. Stuck in a pattern of sin. Stuck in the word failure. Where guilt says, "You've done wrong, leaving the opportunity to change," shame says, "You *are* wrong." Shame seeks to make claims about our identity, even claiming our identity.

The question in this story is not whether or not she is guilty. Recognizing guilt can help us correct course, ultimately leading us to forgiveness and redemption. But shame is different. Allowing shame to become our new identity is exceedingly harmful. Writing this spoken word—trying to see this situation from this woman's perspective—was emotional. I can't identify with her situation specifically, but we have all sinned, leaving us vulnerable to the stuckness of shame.

It only takes three chapters into the Bible for sin and shame to appear. The fall of humanity occurred with lies laced with truth. The temptation within a question. "Did God really say you can't eat from the tree in the Garden?" (Genesis 3:1 CSB). Satan, known as the accuser and thief, brought/brings confusion. The story goes on as both Adam and Eve ate the forbidden fruit, and for the first time, the pain of the weight of sin and shame entered the world. One moment stole the perfection intended and brought guilt. Only innocence was known before this moment. With those bites, sin and shame entered. Adam and Eve would try to cover their shame, recognizing their nakedness. They tried to hide from God when they heard His voice. This scene in the garden lives on today. Satan is still the accuser. He is the thief trying to steal peace, identity, and abundant life. He is a confuser, taking truths and lacing them with lies, causing questions when God brings clarity.

The good news is found in one name alone: Jesus! His blood paid the ransom. He is the giver of life. His words are clear. As Adam and Eve tried hiding from God in the garden, He pursued them. The love of God is a beautiful pursuit. In the garden, as Adam and Eve reveal their shame, God provides them with a covering. Though this covering is temporary, it is the beginning of the story of redemption—the first sacrifice as He provided animal skin to cover their nakedness. Eventually, the ultimate, once and for all, sacrifice would happen as Jesus would pay our ransom of sin with his death on the cross. We cannot work our way to redemption, but Jesus' one work has provided redemption. The Bible tells this big, beautiful love story.

The Scene Study

- Put yourself in the scene. How does your life change after this moment?

  - How does your life change if you are an onlooker?

  - How does your life change if you are a Pharisee?

  - How does your life change if you are the woman?

- What was revealed to you about Jesus through this story?

- Spend some time reading and re-reading the story in scripture. Ask for a new revelation. Sit in silence and listen. Journal your thoughts. How is God speaking to you? What is your takeaway from this story? Draw what you feel or write a poem or a prayer.

The Senses

- If you can, find some sand. You can find sand at a playground, sand at the beach, or simply some dirt in your backyard. What sin or word or failure or narrative are you carrying with you? Write it in the sand. Pray over it. Release it to Jesus. Ask for forgiveness if forgiveness is needed. Ask for restoration and healing. Authentically talk to Jesus.

- Now, Erase that word. Hold a handful of sand in your hand. And begin counting the sand! It is impossible! There are millions of tiny grains of sand in your hand that would be impossible to count with the human eye. Soak in the truth of scripture. Psalm 139: 17 - 18, "God, how precious your thoughts are to me; how vast their sum is! 18 If I counted them, they would outnumber the grains of sand; when I wake up, I am still with you." (CSB)

- Now, look at the sand in your hand again. If God's thoughts for you equaled just your handful of sand, they would be so vast in number it would be impossible to count. But God is so much bigger than we could ever imagine. His thoughts for you outnumber the grains of sand on the earth. Look at the sand in front of you; His thoughts are more. Now add the sand in the deepest parts of the ocean that we cannot see. His thoughts are more. Now add the sand in the desert. His thoughts are more. Now, add the sand to every playground.

His thoughts are more.... Are you grasping this truth? His thoughts for you are impossible to count. They are infinite. A love that is beyond our complete comprehension because it is so vast. Let that settle in your heart! The God who created the sand you are holding, the view you are seeing, also created you! You are His masterpiece.

- Now, wherever you are, in that same sand, write a truth about who you are! A truth to combat the shame. A truth to replace the failure. A truth from the Bible of who you are in God's eyes. Perhaps you need to embrace God's forgiveness and, in turn, forgive yourself. Therefore, the word you may need to write is "forgiven." The word may be redeemed. The word may be a child of the King. Perhaps you've felt lost, but you now realize you are found! Maybe the world has made you feel unworthy, but you now proclaim that you are a priceless masterpiece of God the Creator! You are fearfully and wonderfully made! You were created on purpose! You have a purpose!

- Savor this moment with Jesus! Embrace the truth! Remember and hold on to the fact that He desires a relationship with you. Grab a little sand and keep it in a jar as a reminder of the truth.

Chapter VIII

The Child

The Scripture

John 6:1 - 15 (CSB)

*1 After this, Jesus crossed the Sea of Galilee (or Tiberias).
2 A huge crowd was following him because they saw
the signs that he was performing by healing the sick.
3 Jesus went up a mountain and sat down there with
his disciples. 4 Now the Passover, a Jewish festival, was
near. 5 So when Jesus looked up and noticed a huge
crowd coming toward him, he asked Philip, "Where
will we buy bread so that these people can eat?" 6 He
asked this to test him, for he himself knew what he was
going to do. 7 Philip answered him, "Two hundred*

denarii worth of bread wouldn't be enough for each of them to have a little." 8 One of his disciples, Andrew, Simon Peter's brother, said to him, 9 "There's a boy here who has five barley loaves and two fish—but what are they for so many?" 10 Jesus said, "Have the people sit down." There was plenty of grass in that place; so they sat down. The men numbered about five thousand. 11 Then Jesus took the loaves, and after giving thanks he distributed them to those who were seated—so also with the fish, as much as they wanted. 12 When they were full, he told his disciples, "Collect the leftovers so that nothing is wasted." 13 So they collected them and filled twelve baskets with the pieces from the five barley loaves that were left over by those who had eaten. 14 When the people saw the sign he had done, they said, "This truly is the Prophet who is to come into the world." 15 Therefore, when Jesus realized that they were about to come and take him by force to make him king, he withdrew again to the mountain by himself.

At Rise

This miracle is accounted for in all four gospel books. Each tells the same story, and each provides little details to the story. John's passage offers a precise detail. This miracle meal came from a boy's lunch.

John's account also points to a massive detail. This miracle occurred surrounding the festivities of Passover, a celebration of God's providence and deliverance for His people. Jesus, the one who would provide the ultimate and final deliverance for all humanity, also physically provided for the people's needs. Mark and Luke's account reveals that the disciples had just returned from their commissioned time of ministry as this day began to unfold. Mark further adds the detail that the disciples were anticipating a day of rest. The parallel account in Matthew 14 reveals several essential details in the story and setting. First, the previous chapter (Matthew 13) ends with Jesus being rejected in His hometown, showing the reality of what Jesus faced during His earthly ministry. The people waited for Him, yet some simply could not see who He was and rejected Him. Chapter 14, Matthew's account of this miracle, begins with an announcement. Jesus' cousin was recently beheaded. Matthew's account of this miracle begins with Jesus seeking solitude. Matthew gives us a view of some very emotional experiences for Jesus: rejection and grief. Remember, though Jesus was fully God, He was also fully man! He felt. Yet as the day breaks, instead of solitude, a multitude met Jesus, and as several of the accounts word it, He had compassion!

The Scene

Okay!

What I'm about to say won't seem real.

But today was the most awesome day!
No really,
It's true.
I'm telling you,
The teacher,
He can do everything they say He can do!

I know what you're probably thinking.
You think I'm just imagining things.
But I'm not.
I promise I'm not!
I saw everything!
Okay, let me just start at the beginning.

I woke up today.
I just wanted to lay in bed.
Stay.
But then, I heard my mom say my name.
You know, In that certain mom kind of way.
So all I did was say,
"Okay...Okay."
It's the way we start every day.

As I started to leave,
My mom said, "Wait."
Ughhh!! Mom!
She kissed my head.
Gave me my lunch;
Fresh fish and some bread.

When I tell you the next part,

You'll probably say I was dreaming.

But I'm not!

I promise!

It's too big for even kid-sized storytelling!

As I walked down the road,

I was walking by the sea,

Suddenly, I saw people walking fast past me.

It was early.

So, whatever was happening, the news had spread quickly.

And all I knew was I needed to see.

So I ran super fast.

Past lots of people.

I did not want to be last.

When I got there, I saw a man and His friends.

The man seemed important.

This must be a special moment.

I had to squeeze by.

I wanted to see Him.

Get as close as I could to His side.

Then I stopped and decided to look around.

WOW!

1, 2, 3...

I couldn't count.

There were so many.

The people just kept gathering.

There were probably a hundred.

No thousands of people trying to see

This man that was now close to me.

I heard Him ask His friends a question.

It's funny because it didn't seem like He had any hesitation.

Or like He needed their explanation.

And you won't believe the question.

He wanted a solution to feed ALL the people who were there.

I think the friends thought they were in an impossible situation.

I know I'm little.

Just a boy.

But this is not an exaggeration.

And then,

It's like I felt this feeling,

Go talk to them.

I wasn't sure what I had to say.

It's not like I had the money to buy food that day.

I'm just a boy anyway.

But I felt like there was something I could do to help find a way.

I was kind of scared,

But somehow, I was brave.

So I reached for one of His friends.

And without knowing what exactly to say,

I said,

"Here! Have my lunch. It's all I have. But the teacher can have it today."

I was kind of afraid of what the friends might say.

What if the laughed in my face?

What if they told me to go away?

But I knew no matter what,

I had to do something.

And I kind of felt that the teacher could do anything,

Even with such a small, little offering.

Then I saw the teacher's eyes look up at me.
He wasn't like other adults –
Thinking kids are annoying or unclean.
His eyes were kind and welcoming.
And even though I'm old enough to know what I gave was not enough,
It's like His eyes were proud and filled with love.
Then the most amazing thing....
It's like for Him, this was nothing.
He took my offering.
And right there,
My lunch began multiplying!

I'm not the only one who saw this miracle.
Ask any of the thousands of people.
They'll tell you I'm not making this up at all.
I didn't want this day to end.
I just wanted to stay by this teacher and stand.
But people were leaving,
Bellies full and....
With leftover food in their hands.

Will the people I tell think this was just pretend?
Oh well, I know what happened with the lunch in my hand.
So, whether people make fun,
Or people believe.
It doesn't matter to me.
I will never forget what He did with my small offering.

The Story

We do not know what brought this boy to the seashore that day. Perhaps he was on errands for his mom to help prepare for the upcoming Passover celebration. It's possible that he was there with his parents. What brought him that day does not really matter. What matters is that he was there, and what happened that day was nothing short of miraculous.

While only one sentence mentions this boy, we can imagine who he might have been: young, curious, filled with wonder, childlike faith, regular child. His lunch, barley loaves specifically, pointed to his family's poor socioeconomic state, which only adds richness to the story. The vital role of a child in this story provides immense depth. One sentence, one mention, uncovers beautiful intentions as the story's details paint the picture of relationship, care, faith, and welcoming.

Let's step away from the child for a second and turn to the relationship between Jesus and His disciples. In fact, go back to the scripture and read just the beginning portion of John's account and see the progression of the conversation. Jesus starts by asking a question. He did not need an answer; this was not for His sake. So, if not for Him, why not simply do the miracle? Isn't the question just a waste of time? Well, what do questions seek? A response, an answer. Just look at the gospels alone and see how often Jesus asks questions. Yes, He tells stories. Yes, He gives sermons, but there is beautiful intentionality as he asks questions, pointing toward His invitation into a relationship. An invitation to be part of the story. Did Jesus need them to accomplish the miracle? NO! But He invited them to take part, think big, and stretch their minds to imagine heavenly-sized possibilities on earth through Him. He came to redeem the broken relationship between God and man. Revealed in this question is a grace-filled invitation for people to join him. Jesus certainly could have fed the crowd without any help. That would be easier and more time-efficient. Instead, Jesus provided an invitation to connection and participation in His Kingdom work. That invitation to join him still exists today. Eternal life through Jesus does not need to wait until we're in heaven. The relationship begins here on earth when we believe in and receive His life-changing redemption.

The story continues. Through the question, we discover that a boy has a lunch of two fish and five pieces of bread. Scripture does not reveal how this young boy and his lunch were singled out to feed over 5,000 people. (On a side note, this number was thought to be much larger as men were the ones counted in the 5,000, but this boy's lunch is up for discussion.) Perhaps the boy was with his family, and they had started talking to one of the disciples. Maybe the boy was alone and, as young kids do, tried to get as close to the situation as possible (being young, small, and agile helps you get through a crowd). Scripture does not give us this detail, but at this moment, the boys' lunch is the best idea the disciples have—which, of course, was in and of itself ridiculous. Thus, Jesus' response to the meager offering of this child would have stood out. We know that Jesus welcomed little children, and we see that here. Another story in Matthew 19:15 demonstrates Jesus' love for children.

Then little children were brought to Jesus for him to place his hands on them and pray, but the disciples rebuked them. Jesus said, "Leave the little children alone, and don't try to keep them from coming to me, because the kingdom of heaven belongs to such as these." After placing his hands on them, he went on from there. (Matthew 19:13 - 15, CSB)

When others may want to put the kids at the children's table or to the side, Jesus welcomes them. Jesus also affirms them and goes so far as to use them as exemplars of true faith.

"Truly I tell you," he said, "unless you turn and become like little children, you will never enter the kingdom of heaven." (Matthew 18:3, CSB)

Why would Jesus tell us to be like children? To have faith like a child is to still believe in the impossible. Imagine the depth and joy of believing wholeheartedly in a God who can do impossible things, not because of an unrealistic thought or fairy tale, but because He can. It is a trust with no reservations. This trust creates a willingness to step into the impossible with Jesus. There is an interesting dichotomy when you read this entire chapter as a boy with an insignificant lunch (it may have fed him, but certainly not a crowd), openhandedly giving everything he had, resulting in a meal of abundance for 5,000 plus people.

Unabandoned faith. Yet, if you read this chapter to the end, after Jesus fed 5,000 people with this lunch, walked on water, and then preached to the people, followers of Jesus began to leave. Why? Because of His hard teaching. At the beginning of John's account, we see Jesus physically provided through the substance of bread and fish. At the end of the chapter, Jesus speaks of spiritual sustenance as He proclaims the first of the seven "I Am" statements in the book of John: "I am the bread of life." (John 6:35 CSB). For context, Jesus stating "I am" was a bold declaration that He was/is God. This reference goes back to Moses and the burning bush in Exodus 3 when God calls Moses to go to Egypt and be part of His plan of deliverance for the people (another invitation to join in on a God-sized plan). Jesus is making this "I am" statement here, as the Passover feast (the feast that celebrates the deliverance from Eqypt found in Exodus) is underway. We might read it today and think Jesus is using proper sentence structure, but the people would have understood the meaning behind the words "I Am." So, He sustained them physically at the beginning of this chapter and then later speaks of spiritual sustenance at the end. His followers accepted the physical, but some of His followers rejected the spiritual statement at the end as He proclaimed His deity. Emphasis on the fact that these were people who had begun following Jesus. Jesus is who He is! We cannot pick and choose who we want Him to be. We must look at all of who He is and how He provides abundantly. So when His teaching got harder, He was rejected by many. His teachings aren't always easy, but they are always good. All of them!

Now, while this generous act of a little boy giving up his lunch is incredible, the miracle rests in the hands in which he placed the lunch. With a meager lunch, this little boy did not give some of what he had, saving a little for himself, just in case Jesus used it all and none was left for him. He gave everything he had! He could not know the entire outcome. The offering would appear like a band-aid fix for the situation. But he didn't let anything stop him from placing everything in Jesus's hands. Maybe the boy just wanted Jesus to have his lunch. Perhaps he just wanted to contribute anything he could. Both of these motivations are brave and beautiful in and of themselves.

And yet, maybe something about Jesus created a crazy idea inside that little boy—that somehow, this man could do something truly amazing with what he had to offer. Whatever brought this lunch to Jesus, the fact is an offering this size would not just feed a few. It would feed a multitude.

Jesus invited the disciples into the moment. Jesus welcomed the little children and even used them as examples of faith. Jesus took something that was not enough and overflowed the situation. Not only was everyone fed, but there were leftovers! That's not just satisfying the hunger for the moment but providing abundantly above and beyond.

Jesus invites us today to have a relationship with him, just like he did with the disciples. He welcomes our conversation and our questions. He invites us to be a part of the kingdom work. He is not just here for one transaction. What would happen today if we offered Him everything, no matter how big or small it seems?

The Backstory

Writing this chapter was different from the rest. There was joy and almost laughter about it. It was fun to imagine this story not just through the eyes of a child but from the child whose lunch fed 5,000+ people.

I remember playing the role of Lucy Van Pelt in the musical "You're A

Good Man Charlie Brown." I was 23 at the time, playing a 5-year-old. Lucy was bossy, cute, crabby, competitive, and an all-around blast of a part to play, especially as an adult. I had a character voice with a different inflection, a higher pitch, and tone. My walk had a kid's bounce to it. At the end of the two-hour play, I was exhausted! Being five is a lot of hard work! From rehearsal to the performances themselves, it was a collective blast back to the past of childhood and the things I had observed in child-like behavior. The world held awe, wonder, excitement, and joy, surrounded by curiosity. The view from a child is beautiful.

Ok, one more story, if that's ok. This story takes us from actor to director. As a director, I savor every moment, from auditions to performances. This particular show for this story came with varying circumstances that were more difficult than usual. Whether a show was spiritually based or not, my directing partner and I always focused on uniting the cast and crew on Jesus. We would do this with occasional prayer and devotions throughout the entire process. At this moment, for this show, we found ourselves needing to restructure the entire show three weeks before opening night. In all reality, opening night felt like an impossibility. We chatted and decided we were moving forward but with a dynamic shift in focus. We were going to tithe our time. What did that mean? Each rehearsal for the next three weeks would begin with us giving our time to Jesus as a cast—our small offering when, realistically, we did not have time to give. Looking back, I am so thankful for the difficulties we faced. Difficulties we did not want to go through, but that brought us to this decision. The difficulty changed me as an artist, well really as a person, for the rest of my life. In the end, the show went on; honestly, it is one of my favorite directorial experiences. It was a powerful show, and as a small cast and crew, we felt like we had seen a miracle occur. Our small offering in the hands of Jesus can multiply miraculously.

The Scene Study

- Place yourself in the shoes of the disciples. What may they have felt as the crowd grew and Jesus was asking an impossible question?

- Describe a time you saw Jesus use an "offering" that was too small to bring about a miraculous result far beyond any expectation.

- Imagine eating that meal. What would you feel? How would it taste as you take your first bite of a miracle meal?

- Describe qualities found in child-like faith?

The Senses

- For one day, try to observe life through the wonder and awe of a child. Take a walk; what do you observe? How do you find joy in little things? Even play a bit, whether engaging with a hobby, playing a game, reading a book, or painting a picture (maybe even with your fingers). The God of all creation knows and loves you and delights in His children. Observe His creation through the eyes of a child. Look for the unique qualities of people you encounter. Try on the belief that God is strong and present in every one of your life circumstances. Write what you observe.

- Practice offering. What small offering can you give? Perhaps it is time serving at your church, or tutoring kids, or feeding the homeless. It could be paying for the lunch of the person in line at the drive-through behind you or buying lunch for a friend to have a quality conversation. Offer something in your life to God, whether time, talent, or treasure, and write your reflection on the experience.

Chapter VIIII

The Bold

The Scripture

M atthew 14:22-33 (CSB)

22 Immediately he made the disciples get into the boat and go ahead of him to the other side, while he dismissed the crowds. 23 After dismissing the crowds, he went up on the mountain by himself to pray. Well into the night, he was there alone. 24 Meanwhile, the boat was already some distance from land, battered by the waves, because the wind was against them. 25 Jesus came toward them walking on the sea very early in the morning. 26 When the disciples saw him walking on the sea, they were terrified. "It's a ghost!" they said, and they cried

out in fear. 27 Immediately Jesus spoke to them. "Have
courage! It is I. Don't be afraid." 28 "Lord, if it's you,"
Peter answered him, "command me to come to you on
the water." 29 He said, "Come." And climbing out of
the boat, Peter started walking on the water and came
toward Jesus. 30 But when he saw the strength of the
wind, he was afraid, and beginning to sink he cried
out, "Lord, save me!" 31 Immediately Jesus reached out
his hand, caught hold of him, and said to him, "You
of little faith, why did you doubt?" 32 When they got
into the boat, the wind ceased. 33 Then those in the
boat worshiped him and said, "Truly you are the Son
of God."

At Rise

Matthew 14 provides a detailed look into a very long day for Jesus, marked by three significant events recorded in Matthew. First, Jesus just found out that his cousin, John the Baptist, had been beheaded. John was not some long-lost cousin that Jesus had never met. John the Baptist was only months older than Jesus, and both were miracle births, one conceived in a barren womb, the other growing in a virgin womb. They were both announced by the same angel, Gabriel. John was the Prophet foretold in Isaiah 40, who would come to prepare the way for Jesus. From the womb, these two cousins had a special bond,

John "leaping" for joy in his mother Elizabeth's womb in response to the voice of Mary, the mother of Jesus (See Luke 1:41). John baptized Jesus in the Jordan River, where the Holy Spirit descended on Jesus, launching him into his earthly ministry (See Matthew 3:13–17, Mark 1:9–11, Luke 3:21–22). Each spoke highly of the other and testified about the calling of the other. John's death was heavy news. As we read in the following chapters, from this moment on, there is a shift of focus to Jesus' upcoming death. The announcement of John's death happened in Matthew 14; Jesus then predicted His death just two chapters later in Matthew 16 and continued to predict it two more times before his arrest in Matthew 26. John prepared the way and is now gone, and Jesus quickly begins to predict His very own death.

As the day began, Jesus sought to withdraw to a remote place, presumably to grieve and pray. Whatever the reason, solitude was not what He found. Instead of solitude, Jesus was ultimately met by 5,000-plus people. His response was action: to heal many of their sick and miraculously feed the multitude with food to spare. Once dinner was over, Jesus sent the disciples ahead of him. They would travel by way of the Sea of Galilee while He took the time to dismiss the crowd and then be alone to pray.

This is the context of our story. Presumably, after several hours of prayer for Jesus and rowing for the disciples, we reach the early morning hours while it is still dark out. The disciples struggled with their journey across the Sea of Galilee, battered by the opposing wind and waves. Imagine a dark night on the water. No flashlights or headlights. No radar or autopilot. It is just you, the moon, the stars, and the water. They were in the darkness, battling a storm of their lives.

The Scene

He told us to cross the sea.
That's nothing to me.
I was a fisherman, you see.
So this should be easy.
He told us to go ahead.
He'd stay behind.
We should leave.

The sea was calm.
At peace.
But the thing about this sea,
Storms can arise quickly,
As the waters shift fiercely.
Let me tell you the story.

This storm came out of nowhere.
Fast and robust like a terror.
The wind began to blow,
As the storm began to grow.
It was unpredictable.
It seemed inescapable.
Impossible.
In an instant, the wind became unbearable.

The darkness had no end.

I could barely see my hand.

Let alone a horizon pointing to land.

Imagine the chaos.

It was a battle that seemed lost.

Not to mention,

A boat full of different conclusions.

Which only created more chaos and confusion –

Multiple solutions.

It was utter commotion,

With rising emotions.

All hope was on the shore of the sea,

Where He stayed behind.

Why did we leave?

I know the sea.

This should have been nothing to me.

So, against the wind, we paddled.

Trying to gain an inch.

Paddle!

Together!

Paddle!

Harder!

This storm cannot win this battle.

We have to keep fighting.

This can't be my ending.

What about my wife, who is at home waiting?

Keep Paddling!

This can't be what I came for,

Why I started following.

Leaving the security of fishing,

To only end up dying!

How could this be the meaning?

Keep Paddling!

But the wind just kept fighting,

As the waves kept crashing.

Then, I looked out at the sea desperately.

What?

No!

I could not believe.

What do my eyes see?

Among the crashing waves,

There was a man on the sea.

Yes, you heard me.

On the sea!

My eyes must be playing tricks on me.

This is an illusion, not reality.

What I think I see simply can't be.

A man walking on water.

Seamlessly.

Effortlessly.

As if He has power over the waves under His feet.

It must be a ghost.

Maybe a dream.

The storm is getting to me,

Making me see things that simply can't be.

Then He spoke

"Have courage. Don't be afraid. It is me."

So I speak,

"Lord, if it is you, call me out onto the sea."

"Come."
One word,
One call,
To come out of the boat.
The storm still surrounded us all.

But I step.
Step into the storm.
One step, then another.
How is it possible?
I'm walking on water!
You have to remember,
Realize,
This was a storm.
This boat was filled with people who feared for their lives.
Everyone working to keep this boat on the upside,
Avoid a capsize.
Screams,
Shouts,
We were horrified.
But I stepped out of the boat
As they yelled,
Terrified.

But I go.
I can't listen to their screams.
I Take a step,
Then another.
I try to focus my eyes.
I'm walking on water!

Storm or no storm,

My feet stepped.

One step, then another.

Eyes locked in on Him.

I stepped closer.

But suddenly I remember,

This is impossible.

I'm on the water.

And just like that, the storm felt stronger.

How?

What?

Why?

My mind began to analyze.

Andin One brief second,

I remembered the storm's size.

Felt the waves.

As fear and doubt compromise my focus.

And for one second, I shift my eyes.

Take them off Him.

That's all it took.

And in an instant, I started to sink.

My mind began to think about the storm.

My faith began to shrink.

Panic.

Flashes of my family and friends.

Heartache.

Thoughts of my wife.

Will I see her again?

Thinking this storm will be my end,
Fear began.
How ironic that the sea would take this fisherman.
But I was just following His command.
Did I misunderstand?
Swallowed now by waves.
I couldn't get the upper hand.
The storm is too strong.
But then I see His hand.
He is reaching down,
Saving me.
In the middle of the storm, He is there to rescue me.
He is stronger than the storm that has overtaken me,
Making me a captive of the sea.
But as He reaches down, He sets me free.
He pulls me out of the sea's captivity.
And in His eyes, compassion, love,
There is security.

And I wonder,
Why did I take my eyes from Him to the sea?
He is more powerful than I can conceive.
It's as though He has power over all things.

He did not leave me.
He reached out His hand to me.
Together, we got into the boat's security;
Out from the waves of the sea.
And then,
Just like that,
Effortlessly,

He calmed the sea.

Peace.

What did I just see?

How easy it is to forget the miracles in the storm.

How easy to sink,

Drown in the darkness that has formed.

Just that day, 5,000 were fed,

From a little boy's lunch,

Just some fish and some bread.

I watched Him meet needs.

I watched a miracle take place.

Yet, in this space,

When darkness surrounded,

The miracle of that day seemed to be erased.

I could only see what was right in front of my face.

I will never forget that night.

The fear, Yes!

But more, how darkness was defeated by His light.

The storm was nothing compared to His might.

The Story

Scripture is full of real, flawed people taking steps of faith on their individual journeys, just as we do daily. What stands out about Peter is his all-in approach. The term "lukewarm" was not in Peter's vocabulary. The stories of Peter demonstrate both epic faith and colossal failures. His stories are not only in the four gospels (Matthew, Mark, Luke, and John), but he continues to be seen throughout the New Testament. He would go on to write the books of 1st and 2nd Peter and profoundly impact the early church (and the church today).

Peter could be described as a bold, passionate, hot-headed, working man. He was a fisherman by trade with his brother Andrew (another disciple of Jesus). Peter was a husband. Peter was a close friend of Jesus (among his closest inner circle). He was talkative, quick to answer, tenacious, a leader, reactive, all-in, and opinionated. The list could go on. He is quite different from the other characters discussed in this book because we have so much more information about who Peter was.

This specific day would have seemed like a never-ending day. Early news of John the Baptist's death had reached Jesus and the disciples. What do you do as a disciple of the Messiah at this moment? Amidst all this, Jesus heads to a remote place close to shore. Instead of finding solitude and quiet, a 5000-plus-person crowd begins to form. Jesus' name was getting more and more known. News of Him was spreading, and people were seeking to be next to Him, to hear from Him, and maybe witness or be the recipient of a miracle. We are told that Jesus had compassion on the crowd and miraculously healed them and provided for their physical needs by feeding them.

It is essential to note the surrounding details of the events just before Peter's bold walk on water. Peter had just witnessed and eaten a miraculous meal. This miracle would be fresh on everyone's mind. Their bellies are full from that miracle. Did the food taste better because it was miraculous? Was the fellowship lively? I don't know about you, but I would be savoring this meal, and I don't even like fish! But if miracle bread and fish were in front of me, each bite would be eaten with fascination, awe, and wonder to last a lifetime. But, how easy it is to forget the miracle that just occurred when the storm strikes.

Once everyone had been fed, Jesus—seeking solitude in prayer—sent His disciples ahead of Him on a boat, taking the sea to their next destination, presumably where He would meet up with them later. As the disciples were separated from Jesus, great winds arose, and waves began to grow. The placement of the Sea of Galilee, surrounded on all sides by hills, allows heavy and fast wind to arise seemingly out of nowhere. The perfect geographical placement for harsh weather conditions. So, what might start as a calm boat ride can quickly turn into a fierce storm.

Now, try to put yourselves in this severe situation the disciples find themselves in. It is early morning, meaning they are likely still covered in darkness. They've been paddling for hours against the wind and waves. Everyone on the boat is trying to stay afloat and live to see another day. The fishermen would have had boating skills, but not all had trades from the sea. The discussion was likely not quiet and calm amongst the storm's violence. I imagine the disciples' voices were probably amplified with complex expressions of fear, adding to the chaos.

Are you picturing it? Then, seemingly out of nowhere, an image began walking towards them on the water! WALKING! Not swimming, not in another boat, walking on water. Are my eyes playing tricks on me? That's the safe question for them to ask. The next question would be, who or what is this? Is this a ghost? Do I believe in ghosts? Am I dead?

Enter fast-acting Peter! He's been there the whole time, but here he was again, the first to step up and talk. Jesus identified Himself, but Peter wanted confirmation for his next steps. So he asked, "If it is you, Lord, command me to come out there?"

Say what? Can you imagine what the other disciple must have thought?

"Peter, what are you thinking?"

"Peter, for once, can you just stay quiet?"

"Are you crazy?"

Or perhaps there was no time for the others to respond as the man walking on water replied to Peter with just one word, "Come."

The scene offers a valuable lesson. Peter sought Jesus, waited for the command to come, and then responded in obedience. It's easy to go forward with our plans without truly seeking Jesus. It can be easy to get an idea, move, and then, as an afterthought, see what God thinks about the plan. But Peter asked, and when Jesus said, "Come," Peter took an incredible step of faith, leaving the boat's safety. Notice that no one else got out of the boat with him. No one else responded in a step of faith. Peter did not let his fears, or the potential fears of others, keep him from obedience. He left the shaky security of the boat into the wildness of the storm.

So, with the storm still raging, Jesus and Peter were now walking on water. Peter took one step of faith at a time; his eyes were focused on Jesus until they weren't. As the impossible happened, his focus shifted from Jesus to the storm around him. With that focus shift, Peter began to sink. It looked like the end for bold Peter—that is, until

Jesus reached down and pulled him up from sure death.

There are so many takeaways from this story. One is to remember the miracles. As a storm approached, the day's miracle was seemingly forgotten; the focus turned to the storm. In the middle of the storms of life, hold onto the miracles that have happened before. "Jesus is the same yesterday, today, and forever" (Hebrews 13:8 CSB).

Peter was the only disciple who got out of the boat and braved the storm. When Jesus called him, he answered. Peter quickly took those steps of faith. He did not second guess (at least at first). Why could Peter even think about possibly getting out of the boat? Well, it for sure was not because of his ability. He could only take those steps on the water because of the one who called him out onto the sea, Jesus. In and of Peter's ability, walking on water was impossible. However, Jesus had already shown His power. He just healed many and provided a miraculous lunch. The only reason Peter could do the impossible was because of Jesus. Did Peter know the outcome of his steps of faith? Did he imagine he would walk on water? Who knows. We do know that steps of faith can be taken when stepping toward the faithful one.

Peter walked, but he also sank due to a switch in focus. It can be easy to shift our focus from Jesus to the storm. He is the author and finisher of our faith—the only constant. Difficulties will come our way. As I write this book, I have felt the weight of triumphs, joys, and life's storms. We must keep our eyes focused on Jesus through it all. Seeing the reality of the life-threatening situation, Peter looked around and shifted his focus to fear and worry, but the world's savior was still standing before him. The creator of the wind and sea was with him. When the storms of this world rage on, remember the creator of this world is mightier than any storm. Keep the correct focus and perspective. Though Peter began to sink, Jesus was still there. Even when we lose focus, like Peter, Jesus is still there. This is a picture of how Jesus walks with us amid the storms of life. Jesus did not condemn Peter or scold Peter. He did not make him wait it out so that he learned his lesson. No! When Peter cried out, "Lord, save me!" Jesus was right there, offering his outstretched hand. Peter would have to focus on his hand and reach for it. When the focus shifts and the storm appears bigger than we can handle, look for the outstretched hand of Jesus somewhere right in front of you. It won't be far off, but we still have to choose to take it.

As I write this chapter, I am listening to California's first hurricane/tropical storm (the final categorization is a little iffy) since 1939. As I am typing, there is a literal storm outside my window, with raging wind and pounding raindrops. I could not let this moment pass without writing about our friend Peter. Storms in life, both figuratively and literally, will come our way. When they do, we can look at Peter's story. Remember the miracles that have happened before. Listen for Jesus' voice in the chaos. Step out in faith even in a storm, and keep our eyes focused on Jesus. When we think Jesus is so far off and can't understand what we are going through, we can look to the beginning of this chapter, where we see Jesus experience the news of his close cousin's brutal death. Remember, Jesus experienced human emotions. He understands. He is there for us. But even if we forget or lose focus, remember He is still there. Find his hand and let him pull you back out.

The Backstory

I don't know about you, but I have a healthy fear of water. Now, that does not mean I won't jump into a lake or go into the ocean. In fact, I love snorkeling and used to surf with my brother in my twenties. Observing an underwater world or feeling the rush of riding a wave is exhilarating. At the same time, I understand that water is powerful. Waves can wipe you out and take you under, upending you and leaving you unsure which way to swim for air. So yes, I love the water, but I also respect the water and its strength.

Let's go on a journey back to my freshman year of high school, where a water adventure would be used to build my faith. Now, I wasn't called out of a boat to walk on water, but I did leave the security of a boat when the water was much stronger than me, as my youth group went on a summer adventure camp. We road-tripped up the coast of California, eventually turning inland into the mountains, where we set up camp settled within the beauty of the American River. Amongst all the adventurous things we were about to do, the part that had me scared to tears as we set out, leaving the security of the church parking lot, were the white water rapids we would face on the river. Yes, you heard me right; I was the freshman girl crying for her mom in front of everyone. However, I was comforted by these words from my youth pastor, "No one ever falls out of the raft." Unfortunately, these would prove to be "famous last words."

Our first day of river rafting came, and I was keenly aware of what was before me. I listened intently to the safety instructions, but almost as quickly as the instructions were given, we were off on our 21-mile adventure. For the first ten minutes, I was tense, but slowly, I began to loosen up and, dare I say, even have some fun. Then, we started our approach to our first class 3 rapid. Now, on a scale of 1 -5, 1 being a swimmer's rapid, 5 being a *waterfall-nice-knowing-you* kind of rapid, a three is strongly in the middle. The guides even named each rapid on the familiar path. The name of the rapid we were approaching was "Meat Grinder." Sounds cute, right? Sarcasm.

As we began the ride into the Meat Grinder, we quickly hit a rock, and I instantly popped out of the raft and into the rapid, all alone! The chaos from the boat began as the guide screamed to get me back in the boat. A frenzy ensued as an oar was extended, but I could not grab it. It was now me and the Meat Grinder alone. Eventually, I gave in and rode the rapid. Fear did not subside at any moment. I felt alone and helpless to the rapid's strength, but I later learned I was not alone and help was there.

Here's my little miracle. You see, I did not hit one rock while bobbing up and down out of control on the rapids of Meat Grinder. The guides were amazed that I did not have one bruise on my body. Once the storm of the moment settled and I could reflect, I realized that God had me in that moment. It was a miracle that I was not injured. I believe that, somehow, the protecting hand of Jesus was extended to me. Did I see His hand? No, but I firmly believe I was miraculously protected. I can still vividly remember this encounter with the water. I could have let the chaos cloud the miracle; I could have focused solely on the water's overwhelming strength; instead, I eventually reflected on the miracle of no injuries. Sometimes, we just need a moment to stop and reflect after the storm and observe the miracle. It does not mean ignoring the storm's existence but recognizing there is one with us in the storm.

The Scene Study

- How do you think this specific moment with Jesus may have impacted Peter's faith?

- What past moments of Jesus' miraculous provision and protection—whether from scripture, your life, or the life of another—can you look to when you are experiencing a storm in this life?

- What are things that might have tried to pull away Peter's focus in the story? What can pull away your focus from Jesus in your own story?

- How can we tangibly keep our attention on Jesus? What can we do in our daily rhythm to refocus our minds and hearts on Him?

The Senses

- Jesus gives the continual example to spend quiet time with God. So take this book, your Bible, perhaps a journal, a sketchpad, a guitar... and find a quiet place. I would suggest finding a space in nature, if possible by the sound of water, and away from the distractions of work or home, and spend time with your Heavenly Father. Talk to him about your joys! Talk to him about your pains and sorrows. Take time to listen to what He may be saying. Pray about that situation you are waiting for. Absorb the beauty of Elohim's creation (God the creator). Respond in writing, drawing, painting, singing, or dancing....Respond in worship!

Chapter X

The Ruler and His Wife

The Scripture

M atthew 27: 15 - 25(CSB)

15 At the festival the governor's custom was to release to the crowd a prisoner they wanted. 16 At that time they had a notorious prisoner called Barabbas. 17 So when they had gathered together, Pilate said to them, "Who is it you want me to release for you—Barabbas, or Jesus who is called Christ?" 18 For he knew it was because of envy that they had handed him over. 19 While he was sitting on the judge's bench, his wife sent word to him, "Have nothing to do with that righteous man, for today I've suffered terribly in a dream because of him." 20

The chief priests and the elders, however, persuaded the crowds to ask for Barabbas and to execute Jesus. 21 The governor asked them, "Which of the two do you want me to release for you?" "Barabbas!" they answered. 22 Pilate asked them, "What should I do then with Jesus, who is called Christ?" They all answered, "Crucify him!" 23 Then he said, "Why? What has he done wrong?" But they kept shouting all the more, "Crucify him!" 24 When Pilate saw that he was getting nowhere, but that a riot was starting instead, he took some water, washed his hands in front of the crowd, and said, "I am innocent of this man's blood.[] See to it yourselves!" 25 All the people answered, "His blood be on us and our children!" 26 Then he released Barabbas to them and, after having Jesus flogged, handed him over to be crucified.

At Rise

This dramatic scene was set in Jerusalem. The streets were more crowded than usual due to the Passover Celebration, the Jewish celebration commemorating the Israelites' deliverance from Egyptian enslavement, found in the book of Exodus. Little did the people know that during this particular Passover, the greatest deliverance of all time was about to take place! One sacrifice to cover all the sins of the whole world for all time.

It is important to note that Jerusalem is now occupied and governed by Rome. So, at the first Passover, the Israelites were enslaved by the Egyptians. Now, here in AD, they are ruled by the Roman Empire. Many hoped that Jesus would come as a warrior to deliver them from Roman occupation, which seemed like an enormous task. Jesus came to deliver the world from so much more. (How often do we only see the small picture before us when God is working on a larger picture at hand?)

Quickly, this time of celebration would turn into a trial and execution. Due to the setting and time, we see a back-and-forth of responsibility. The religious leaders held Jesus first; He was then passed to Pilate. Pilate passed him to Herod, and finally, Jesus ended up back in Pilate's hands as he ultimately, against his wife's request, condemned Jesus, the only wholly innocent, completely pure man, to death.

<u>The Scene</u>

The timing for this conversation is after Pilate has condemned Jesus to death. The scene opens as Pilate is washing his hands and face after a stressful day. During this, his wife enters. There is a question as to whether he had compassion for his wife's dream or was simply dismissive as a cruel ruler. The tension of mixed emotions of husband, arrogant ruler, and the confusion of this crucifixion should be felt. This scene should evoke the complexity of that tension. Pilate hears his wife walk in and turns to talk to her.

PILATE: Well, this is unexpected. What brings you here?

PILATE'S WIFE: Why didn't you listen?

PILATE: What do you mean?

PILATE'S WIFE: You know what I mean. My dream, why didn't you listen to me?

PILATE: This is nothing for you to concern yourself with, my dear.

PILATE'S WIFE: Nothing to concern myself with. How can you say that? You are my husband; of course, I am going to concern myself with the choices you make.

PILATE: Choices! Is that what you think happened today? That I simply made a choice? It was not me. It was them. They made the choice. Not me.

PILATE'S WIFE: But you are the governor.

PILATE: Yes, I realize that! I need no further reminder on a day like today. I mean, did you hear them?

PILATE'S WIFE: Yes, I heard them...But...

PILATE: And as for him...

PILATE'S WIFE: Don't you see it's him I worry about, not the screams of the masses.

PILATE: Yes, but it is the masses who will cause a riot. That is what I am worried about.

PILATE'S WIFE: But what if he is who he says he is?

PILATE: And who do you think he is? Do you think he is this king they talk about? That could cause a whole new situation. A riot even.

PILATE'S WIFE: Didn't he say that he was!? Why would he lie about something that would put him to death? That would be foolish.

PILATE: All he said when asked, "Are you the king of the Jews?" is, "You have said so." I mean, really, is that even an answer?

PILATE'S WIFE: It is an answer! He must be who he says he is.

PILATE: Then why go silent? When I brought the accusations from the chief priests...Why go silent? It makes no sense.

PILATE'S WIFE: Why, except that he is, and deep down, I think you all know he is. He could have said no, and this would all be over. Instead, he was quietly condemned. Don't you see, he must be...

PILATE: Don't finish! I am getting a headache just listening to this.

PILATE'S WIFE: Pilate, if only you had been the one to have the dream.

PILATE: I wish I had then...

PILATE'S WIFE: I wish you had too. For surely you would not have hung that man from a tree, flogged him, let them put a crown of thorns on his head, let them mock him, had YOU been the one to see what I saw in the dream. It terrifies me.

PILATE: It was just a dream.

PILATE'S WIFE: I cannot believe that! I will not believe that! The suffering it caused.

PILATE: There there...

PILATE'S WIFE: Do not patronize me! Do not try to comfort me now. You could have listened to me. Now, who knows what will be?

PILATE: It will all be over soon.

PILATE'S WIFE: And that is what I fear.

PILATE: (Angered) But what would you have had me do? Tell the world that my wife had a dream, and therefore, this man is free. I would be the laughingstock. It would ruin me, or worse, I'd be taken by that mob. They wanted this man's blood so badly that they set a rebel free. Don't you see I tried, and instead, they freed Barabbas, the worst of the worst. Have you thought about that?

PILATE'S WIFE: Yes, I have thought about that and...

PILATE: There is no "and"! That is it! No more.

PILATE'S WIFE: Tell me you think he is guilty; tell me those words, and I will never bring it up again.

PILATE: I cannot.

PILATE'S WIFE: You admit it.

PILATE: I don't know what to think of it.

PILATE'S WIFE: You looked in his eyes! You saw something different about him, didn't you?

PILATE: I said I don't know what to think! All I do know is that there was no other choice to be made, which is why this conversation is over.

PILATE'S WIFE: But Pilate...

PILATE: No! No more! That crowd, I have never heard the yells so loud. The words continue to ring in my head, "Crucify him, crucify him, crucify him..." If I'd let him go, they would have crucified me.

PILATE'S WIFE: Perhaps.

PILATE: Is that all you can say? Perhaps.

PILATE'S WIFE: I did not mean anything by it. But you are the governor, who holds authority...But this man. Pilate, we've seen so many crucifixions; this one is different. What if he is who he said he is? What if he was this king? What if he was more than just a king on this earth? What if?...

PILATE: Enough! This is going nowhere. What's done is done! It is time for us to move on. Wash ourselves of this place. Of this scene! We will soon forget.

PILATE'S WIFE: No. I do not think we will ever forget.

PILATE: We will forget! This one is not on me. It is not on us. It is on those people. They wanted his blood, which is why I took the water and washed my hands of this situation. I am done with this man. His blood is not on me! His blood is on them.

PILATE'S WIFE: No, my dear, I am afraid His blood is on all of us.

Pilate exits angered.

The Story

Stories of Pilate are found in all 4 of the gospels. In addition, historical documents from that time confirm Pilate as governor over this region during Jesus' ministry and death. Pilate is known in history for being a cruel ruler, at times even going through with harsh executions before proper trials occurred. Words given in a character description for Pilate could include ruler, authoritarian, harsh, proud, and power hungry. But at this moment, the following words could be added to his list: unsure, hesitant, afraid, cowardly, conflicted.

What occurred during the harsh punishment of crucifixion? An actual crucifixion is dramatically different from the images we think of displayed on pretty jewelry or wall decorations today. This form of execution was harsh, painful, and long. As if being nailed to a cross was not enough, the ultimate killer in crucifixion was suffocation. The whole body needed to lift up to allow one's diaphragm to expand, allowing a breath to be taken in. Imagine the pain and energy involved in simply breathing. Some would hang on these crosses for hours or even days before succumbing to death; humiliatingly displayed outside the city walls for all entering to see and be warned.

But for Pilate (and his wife), crucifixion would, to some degree, be a normal event, especially if he was quick to execute as history tells it. Yet, somehow, this man, in front of Pilate, was different. This man (Jesus) was causing the Roman leader to question himself. Instead of a quick judgment, he tried three times, in three different ways, to pass on the responsibility and/or appease the people without actually executing Jesus.

What made this crucifixion different? What was it about this man that paused the cruel ruler?

Another character needs to be analyzed before the questions are answered—Pilate's wife. Scripture does not tell us too much about her other than the fact that she had a dream that terrified her, and she begged Pilate not to go through with the execution of Jesus. What did she see in her dream? Did she see images of the miracles that he had done? Did she see his real might as not just human but divine? Did she see a blameless man? What would cause her to be terrified? Was she numb to crucifixions until this moment?

And while she is the governor's wife, she is still a woman in a male-dominated society. Depending on their marriage, this moment could carry great boldness. If her husband was cruel, did this moment of action take great courage on her part? Was she afraid? Or did Pilate have a soft spot for his wife? These are all character-building questions to consider for both of these figures.

While the answers to some of the character questions may not be clear, what is clear is what matters. Pilate is about to take a centerstage role in the scene that sets all the captives free from this moment on. These questions simply help us to consider more deeply the most pivotal moment in history, one that takes place right before Pilate's eyes, through his command.

During this Passover celebration, the Jewish leaders brought Jesus to Pilate. The intention was for Pilate to sentence Him to death. The cruel enforcer clearly does not want to have this man's blood on his hands. He tries to hand the decision over to Herod. That doesn't work. He offers the release of a prisoner. Jesus or Barabbas. Barrabas, an insurrectionist rebel whose crime also included murder. When that does not work, Pilate tries to appease their need for this man's blood by having Jesus flogged nearly to death, a plan that also fails. So, to quench the bloodthirsty mob, he gives in to the wishes and sentences Jesus to death. I encourage you to read all four gospel accounts (Matthew, Mark, Luke, and John) of the crucifixion.

As Pilate, the cruel enforcer, sentenced Jesus to death, he also stated that "this man's blood was washed from his hands." Why would he care? The blood of so many would already be on his hands, but he wanted nothing to do with the death of Jesus.

Pilate could not honestly know his role in history, that he just sentenced Jesus, the Messiah, whose blood would be our final deliverance, offered to everyone who believes and receives this gift. Yes, Pilate just allowed the very one who is offering salvation, even to his executioners, even to him, to be crucified.

What would that night look like for Pilate and his wife? Would they argue? Would there be fear? Did Pilate try to numb the thoughts swirling in his mind? Would images of Jesus now haunt him in his dreams? We can only speculate with others who have thought about this.

The drama above is a simple reflection on what a conversation between husband and wife might have looked like after all was said and done. Some say that Pilate committed suicide (some theorize it was a forced suicide by the Romans), and some say he went on to be a Christian. There are several theories for the mysterious end of Pilate's life. However, we do know that the free gift of salvation even applied to the one who sentenced the savior to death. That is the power of one moment with Jesus and how far Jesus' grace extends.

So, did this day change the trajectory of Pilate's life? There is no firm answer, but it only takes one moment with Jesus to change everything. Here is what we can firmly learn from this story, even without knowing what happened next. This is a story of choice, and that same choice exists today.

Pilate's wife had a choice. Do I believe in this dream and that this man is powerful, or do I ignore Him? In a society where a woman's voice held little importance, she had a choice to stay safe and keep her dream to herself or to take a risk and speak up.

The Religious Leaders had a choice. Do we find freedom in the world's way, accepting Barabas, or do we find freedom in the Way, the Truth, the Life, Jesus? Do we release our pride and self-righteousness and recognize our need for a savior?

The disciples had a choice. Stay committed when the going gets tough, or reject Jesus when the world seems against Him? Stay or flee? Though many did flee, we also see Jesus' grace. They may have had a moment of weakness, but they also went on to spread the good news of Jesus. Failure should not hold us back from being used by God.

Pilate had a choice. He tried to pass the choice to others three times.

He tried to let Herod make the choice. He tried to appease the people, offering a seemingly worse criminal so they would make the choice. He tried to appease one last time through an act he thought would be enough by beating Jesus so close to the point of death, but it wasn't enough. Ultimately, Pilate had a choice. He could no longer pass the responsibility to somebody else. He had to choose for himself. Did he fear Jesus or the mob of people more? Pilate had a choice.

We have that same choice today. Do we risk social standing to believe all of who Jesus is and share that? Do we want a worldy savior or the Savior of the world? Do we stand in faithful strength with Jesus even when the world is against us or the difficulties in life seem too hard, so we hide? Do we try to pass the decision off to someone else, try to do enough, or be enough? Do we choose to put our trust in Jesus, or do we put our trust in the world because it is scary to go against the worldly mentality?

The choice is ours. Jesus does not force Himself on us. He pursues, but in the end, it is an individual choice. Pilate looked Jesus in the eyes, spoke to him, and eventually sentenced Him to death. More substantial than even a death sentence is the fact that Jesus came to conquer sin and death. The offer of Jesus' Saving grace is more powerful than any earthly powerful ruler. So, as Pilate looked into Jesus' eyes, he looked into the eyes of the only one who could save him—the savior of the world. Jesus' love extends out to everyone, yes, even Pilate. It all comes down to a choice: accept this free gift or reject it.

The Backstory

I always imagined Pilate as a villain, but writing the scene above and then directing two incredible actors for a "Stations of the Cross" event opened my eyes to the humanity and complexity of this moment for this man and his wife. I read Scripture and researched. I wanted to understand Pilate, his wife, and her dream. Then I began to write.

Sometimes, the writing process can take an extended time. Other times, the process is quick, inspiration flowing so fast that my fingers can't keep up with the words. This was one of those latter times. Then came the time to hand the script off to the actors. It is one of the most vulnerable moments for me as a writer. I quickly start questioning the words I've written, wondering if they make sense. But for this pre-Easter event, I felt confident that the actors, my friends, involved would handle the words with care. So I handed the script to my friends and we met for our first rehearsal. The whole rehearsal process was incredible as we discussed the intentional movements they would make and how each line would be delivered. We worked as a team to consider how we could show the relationship of this particular husband and wife. How would this disagreement affect their marriage? What was the power dynamic? How might things have gone? We talked through Pilate's wife's dream. What might it have been filled with? Why did it so impact her?

The rehearsal process was filled with rich discussion. While I still felt anger towards this man who condemned my Lord, I did not look at him now as some far-off, villainous figure. I felt a struggle, a conflict, and truly began to wonder what it was like for Pilate to stand face-to-face with Jesus. Watching my friends play these roles was incredibly impactful. Tears streamed down the actor playing Pilate's eyes as he relived the crowd crying, "Crucify Him!" Pilate's story displays choice. It is a reminder that even Pilate, whether he accepted it or not, is someone Jesus died for.

The Scene Study

- Why do you think Pilate tried three times to dissuade the Jewish leaders? What do you think he saw in Jesus?

- We may not know the answers to Pilate and his wife's life after Christ's crucifixion, but we can know how this moment has changed our lives. How has your life changed as you get to know who Jesus is? Whether you have known him for a long time or whether this book is your first encounter with Jesus, how has getting to know Him more changed your life?

- What choices do you see made by the various people observing this moment? And what do you see in those choices?

  ○ The religious leaders

  ○ Pilate's Wife

  ○ Pilate

  ○ The followers of Jesus

The Senses

- Broken pieces! The death and resurrection of Jesus provides deliverance for all humanity. Jesus is the rescuer of our sins. The innocent sacrifice who took our place. Why? Because He loves us! It's that simple. In Him, we are made into new creations. A beautiful art form that displays the beauty of the Good News of Jesus is a Japanese art known as Kintsugi. Each of us has sinned. We all have elements of pain, questions, hurt, brokenness. While our stories are different, they are similar in the fact that we are all flawed, imperfect people. It levels the playing field. Kintsugi takes old things and makes things new.

○ Take a piece of pottery, place it in a plastic bag, or cover it with a towel, and break it. Yes, you heard correctly—break it. (I recommend hitting it only once with a hammer.)

○ You will see unique broken pieces.

○ Now, take your time putting these pieces back together. You can go simple and use hot glue or elaborate with resin and gold to piece the broken art back together.

○ Kintsugi restores something broken with gold resin, creating new beauty.

○ As you put each piece back together, imagine Jesus' healing touch. Imagine the redemption found in His blood. Think of the victory we can declare—not because of anything we have done, but because of what He has done.

○ Pray, talk to Jesus, and work through the brokenness.

○ In the end, observe your new creation of pottery. It is beautiful and unique. No other piece will look exactly like it.

• Reflect and write. If you have accepted Jesus, you are new. If I haven't, now is a great time. Jesus loves you. The Bible says, "For God loved the world in this way: He gave his one and only Son, so that everyone who believes in him will not perish but have eternal life." (John 3:16 CSB). Pray to him and say something like this. "Jesus, I believe you came, lived, died, and rose again because you love me. I believe that you are the King. I ask you to forgive me of my sins. Thank you for the blood you shed to take my place. Thank you that I can be made new, not because of anything I have done but because of your work. Come into my life. Be Lord. "

- Reflect and write what it means to be a new creation in Jesus!

- You are His masterpiece!

- If you said that prayer or your version, share it with a Christ-follower you know. Celebrate! This is the most important choice you could make.

Chapter XI

The Doubter

The Scripture

J ohn 20: 19 - 31

19 When it was evening on that first day of the week, the disciples were gathered together with the doors locked because they feared the Jews. Jesus came, stood among them, and said to them, "Peace be with you." 20 Having said this, he showed them his hands and his side. So the disciples rejoiced when they saw the Lord. 21 Jesus said to them again, "Peace be with you. As the Father has sent me, I also send you." 22 After saying this, he breathed on them and said, "Receive the Holy Spirit. 23 If you forgive the sins of any, they are forgiven them;

if you retain the sins of any, they are retained." 24 But Thomas (called "Twin"), one of the Twelve, was not with them when Jesus came. 25 So the other disciples were telling him, "We've seen the Lord!" But he said to them, "If I don't see the mark of the nails in his hands, put my finger into the mark of the nails, and put my hand into his side, I will never believe." 26 A week later his disciples were indoors again, and Thomas was with them. Even though the doors were locked, Jesus came and stood among them and said, "Peace be with you." 27 Then he said to Thomas, "Put your finger here and look at my hands. Reach out your hand and put it into my side. Don't be faithless, but believe."28 Thomas responded to him, "My Lord and my God!" 29 Jesus said, "Because you have seen me, you have believed. Blessed are those who have not seen and yet believe."

At Rise

This iconic moment in history—the image of which may appear next to "doubt" in the dictionary—occurred after what seemed like complete and utter defeat. The prologue to this defining moment sets this scene of doubt. In a matter of days, the events leading up to this encounter would take those closest to Jesus on a rollercoaster of emotions. What did Thomas observe throughout that monumental week?

Jerusalem would have been abuzz, bursting at the seams, as people arrived from near and far to celebrate Passover. The people lined the streets to adore and praise Jesus (John 12:12–18). The timing of Jesus' praised entrance into the city could not have been more idyllic. This triumphant entry for Jesus fulfilled a prophecy in Zechariah 9:9 that Thomas would know. The man you have followed, trusted, and admired was finally getting the recognition He deserved. Imagine the anticipation for what might be next. The thoughts and excitement swirling around. Would Jesus finally take His rightful place of authority and reveal himself as the Messiah to the masses? It seemed like the perfect coronation for the promised King of Israel was about to take place.

The week, however, took an unexpected turn. It started with a few confusing comments, Jesus seemingly saying He had to die (John 12). Then, during the Passover dinner amongst Jesus' closest friends, Jesus washed everyone's feet as though He was a servant (John 13). What thoughts and feelings would Thomas have felt? Perhaps confusion? Maybe discomfort as Jesus came to him, touching Thomas' dirty feet, massaging free the dirt and grime? The story continues in John 13; during dinner, Jesus revealed that one of the 12 would betray Him. Betrayal? But Jesus was just publicly praised and treated like royalty. At dinner, Jesus taught many things and again alluded to going somewhere, somewhere you cannot come. (See John 13:33) After dinner, Jesus took Thomas and the others to pray with Him in the Garden of Gethsemane (Matthew 26:36-46). From a distance, anguish was the observation. But tired, the disciples fell asleep.

The scene then took a dramatic shift as Judas—one of the twelve, one of Jesus' friends, someone Thomas and the others walked beside for years—arrived with a large mob (John 18). As they went to arrest Jesus, Simon, a friend and a leader, struck at them with a sword. Tensions flared, but again, there was a surprise as Jesus rebuked Simon and gave himself over to be arrested, also healing the injured soldier. From there, most of the disciples scattered.

As dawn broke, rumors swirled of Jesus being taken before the religious leaders (Matthew 26:57-68), Pontus Pilate, Herod, and eventually back to Pilate, where a screaming crowd cried for Jesus to be crucified (Luke 23). This was not how things were supposed to go. In a matter of days, the crowd's response to Jesus went from celebration to execution. Hope dwindled.

This is a possible interpretation of how Thomas might have felt and experienced the moments leading up to his defining doubt. The events are sure. They happened. The feelings are possible, even understandable, when considering the entirety of the week. A perfect storm of confusion, doubt, fear, and shame had been set. The man Thomas had been following for three years was now dead. Imagine the fear of Friday, the dark feeling of defeat that Saturday. And when the joy of Sunday arrived, and the resurrected Jesus was revealed, Thomas was nowhere to be found.

The Scene

Dear Friend,

I write to you today wholeheartedly.

I know you've probably heard of me.

When people think of doubt, they think of me.

It's usually all anyone sees.

Defined by one moment.

It's okay.

I know "doubting Thomas" is realistically who I am known to be.

But perhaps after today,

You'll see,

I was just responding honestly.

Why am I known as a doubter?

Because I wanted proof.

But can I pose a thought?

If you were there,

You may have wanted it too.

For one second, perhaps just put yourself in my head

Remember,

All I knew was my friend was dead.

That whole week was so confusing.

One moment, they were singing Hosanna to Him.

The next moment, they're screaming crucify Him.

How could they turn on Him?

If only they saw what I saw in Him.

He was my friend.

I had so much hope for Him.

Hope In Him.
How can this be how it ends?

I followed Him loyally.
Now, what am I supposed to believe?
Do I remember the miracles I got to see?
Are they stronger than the doubt forming inside of me?
Right now, all I can see is this depressing reality.

Why did this happen?
What did this mean?
How could they hate Him?
Had He not proved to be the long-awaited king?
Or was it all just a dream?

But It was finished.
Everything we had done seemed to diminish.
It felt like my life was finished.
Was it all for waste?
Did I imagine the things I saw You do?
What is the truth?

He died on a Friday.
Hopelessness filled Saturday.
Some went to His tomb on Sunday.
Then, later that day,
They told me an unbelievable miracle happened while I was away.
They told me He was alive.
Was this a sick joke they were trying to play?
And so when I heard the news, I had to debate.

"You tell me He's alive.

Am I supposed to just believe?

I can't!

It's too much.

Think about what you are asking of me.

He died.

He's gone

Just leave it be!

If you want me to believe,

Then, with my own eyes, I need to see.

Let me see His scarred hands.

My hand on His hand.

Let me touch His pierced side.

I need proof of this resurrection.

Remember, on Friday, He died."

That was the conversation.

But there's more to my hesitation.

I wasn't there when the others saw Him.

Left in my isolated questions.

My comprehension could not fathom this incredible depiction.

I was left in the darkness of depression.

Did I want it to be true?

Yes!

But how could I once again put all my hope in You?

What was I supposed to do?

Just blindly trust that what they said was true?

And what about my life now?

If I do,

Would my life be in danger, too?

I needed proof!

And then my life changed in an instant.

Why was I surprised?

This moment was so consistent.

While I doubted what had happened,

While I needed proof.

Eight days later, there He stood.

He extended His hands,

Said, "Touch my side".

He was there.

He was Fully Alive!

This has to be a dream.

You died!

But He was right in front of me.

I could not doubt what my eyes could see.

But they killed Him on that tree.

So when they told me He was alive,

They were words I just couldn't receive.

The pain was too much for me.

But Jesus, you really are here with me!

Why did I not just believe?

His reaction was full of compassion.

He invited my questions.

My friend, Jesus, where my hope can truly rest in,

He didn't leave me in my doubt.

Instead, He leaned in.

So now, instead of giving in,

I will not let doubt become my name.

Instead, Jesus, it is You I will proclaim.

The name above all names.

Please know that for you it is the same.
Doubt will inevitably, at times, arise.
In the chaos, it can feel like hope dies.
Take it from me,
My doubt denied the hope they spoke of on that Sunday Sunrise.
But I now know, beyond a shadow of a doubt,
I fully recognize,
Because I looked directly into His resurrected eyes.

He met me in my doubt.
And while I needed to see Him physically,
I know how special it is for those who have faith but may not get to
see.
In this broken world, when you feel doubt,
Think of me, the one they call "doubting."
A name perhaps of which I am deserving.
But maybe now you have a new understanding.

Learn from me a lesson.
In your doubt, lean into Him.
Don't let your doubt take you on a path away from Him.
He welcomes you and your questions.
It's because He's not here for just a transaction.
A relationship is His intention.

The things of the world
The logic you think you see
It can cause you to think yourself away from who you know Him to
be.

So, in your questions,

In your doubt,

When the world seems inside out,

Let Him walk beside you.

Let His nail-scarred hands comfort you.

Remember, He is always there for you!

I hope my story impacts you!

Not because of me

But because of everything, I saw Him do!

Sincerely

Your Friend

Honest Thomas

The Story

Doubting! It is not the adjective a person hopes for as their legacy, yet here we find Thomas as the poster boy for doubt. But does this one word wholly define him? Or does one day overshadow everything else for Thomas? A single-moment character analysis for Thomas could be doubter, pessimist, unbelieving, realist, fearful, skeptic... Point made. This description is one-dimensional, based on one moment, one day, one reaction. It seems unfair. The truth is, it can be so easy to label ourselves or others after one moment only. When we step back and observe the horrific nature of Friday, the pain, confusion, and fear he would have been experiencing, it is not hard to identify with Thomas.

He quite literally lost all hope. Jesus, the one he left everything to follow, was dead, according to him. To believe anything otherwise would seem like false hope. When hope feels lost, it is easy to experience fear, doubt, and questions. We need to remember that questions are not bad. It is how we posture ourselves in our questions that will have a significant impact on the end of the story. So perhaps there is more to Thomas than meets the eye. For fun, let's look beyond this one moment that seems to define Thomas and observe all of him.

Thomas takes a speaking role three times in Scripture, though he is mentioned more. Looking at Thomas holistically could even change his name from "Doubting Thomas" to "Loyal Thomas". How's that for a dramatic shift? And yet, here we are, 2,000 plus years later, still remembering him simply as "Doubting Thomas." So who was Thomas? It seems fitting to ask a lot of questions for Thomas, as he was someone who asked questions and sought physical evidence!

In John 11, we see Thomas' loyalty and boldness in the famous story of Jesus raising Lazarus from the dead. Lazarus and his sisters were not simply acquaintances or people Jesus met once. These three siblings were some of Jesus' dearest friends. The sisters pleaded for Jesus to come and heal their sick brother. Now, to journey to Lazarus would mean returning to Judea, where the people had tried to stone Jesus on a previous trip. Understandably, this might seem like a time for questions and concerns to arise, but not from Thomas.

The disciples were asking questions and making statements such as, "If he is sleeping, let him sleep " or "Don't you remember that the people there are trying to kill you, and now you want to go back?" (John 11:8 -11). Thomas, however, boldly states, "Let's go too so that we may die with him." (John 11:16). So much for doubt and fear.

Jesus' life was being threatened, and going to Lazarus would inevitably put Jesus and the disciples in the middle of the threat. Amongst the danger, Thomas says, "Charge." "Onward!" " Let's go!" It's as though there was no question of belief and only the question of "when we are going?" *Where Jesus goes, I go*, seems to be the mentality. There was a fierce commitment to who he was following! So much for doubt.

The next time we hear from Thomas is in John 14. At the Last Supper, before Jesus' death, Jesus told His disciples that He would be leaving and going to prepare a place for them, but they knew the way to where He was going. Thomas quickly spoke up and asked, "Lord…We don't know where you are going. How can we know the way?" (v. 5 CSB). Jesus responded, "I am the way, the truth and the life, no one comes to the Father except through me. If you know me, you also know my Father. From now on you do know Him and have seen Him." (John 14: 6- 7 CSB). Read the whole account! It's good!

Thank you, Thomas, for asking your question. Even today, we still get to embrace and cherish these words from Jesus. Words that point to Jesus being the only way of salvation. Thomas's question reveals fierce loyalty, a longing to be near Jesus, and an urgency to know precisely how to find Jesus when He left.

When these two moments are added to Thomas' character analysis, depth and dimension emerge. If I were writing a play based on Thomas' story, some of the words I would use in Thomas' character description, when looking at his whole person, would be bold, fiercely loyal, investigator, realist, faithful friend, willing to go against the popular vote, seeker. So why is doubting the one word we remember? Well, let's be honest: it is much easier to remember the less-than-perfect moments of our stories or other's stories. This can stop us from moving forward in life. But what happens when Thomas is given a new name? What happens when we call him "Honest Thomas?" It changes everything!

Thomas seemed open and honest about his thoughts and so loyal that he wanted to know the answers because he wanted to be near Jesus. What a wonderful place to want to always be, near Jesus. So, what happened here if Thomas was previously fearless in asking questions or going against popular opinion? Well, for one thing, by not simply going with the flow and seeking answers for himself, he is staying true to what was seen earlier in scripture. He boldly went against the flow, even if it was the truth and the answer he hoped for. He was honest.

Thomas was not with the other disciples when Jesus first revealed His resurrected body.

Where was he? Now I'm the one with the questions. Was he isolating himself? Was it too hard to be with these friends? Was the once bold Thomas afraid for his life? Did he feel lost after the death of the one in whom his hope was placed? Was it a simple answer, like he was the one out getting dinner for everyone else? Where was Thomas? The truth is, we do not know why he was not there initially, but having doubts while away from other believers can be scary. We must also re-member that these friends telling Thomas this incredible news are his most trusted friends. These are the people who were following Jesus during His earthly ministry. Together, they were first-hand witnesses to the miraculous. Together, they heard the teachings of Jesus. To-gether, they walked with Jesus. These are not random people claiming this miracle resurrection. Thomas' closest friends were united on this amazing news, but Thomas still does not believe it. It's not just that they are united, but what and who they were united on. Jesus had predicted His death and resurrection. The disciples may not have fully understood while He made the predictions, but He spoke about this. So, the disciples were united on the words of Jesus having come true. That is the key. We can unite on the wrong thing, which can lead to destruction, or we can unite on the word of God, in this case, the literal words they heard from Jesus. That is uniting on absolute truth. These are words that Thomas would have heard as well, but he still could not believe it, even though his friends were united on the truth.

Thomas seems like one with deep faith and trust in Jesus! Then Jesus died! Literal darkness came over that place, and the earth shook. Imagine the emotions and confusion; the person you had put all trust and hope in was now dead. The paradigm shift in thinking would have been extreme. It is easy to find ourselves stuck in the darkness with questions, feeling hopeless. Imagine the waiting on Saturday before Sunday came. Place yourself in the disciple's shoes. Those days between the death of Jesus and His resurrection had to be filled with extreme darkness and pain. If only Thomas would have remembered the answer to his early question. "How will we know to find you?" and Jesus replied, " I am the way, the truth, and the life. No one comes to the Father except through me." Jesus had answered the question, but how easy it is to forget when smack dab in the middle of the darkness. It is easy to get stuck in the question instead of looking to the one who holds the answers. It is easy to go down the rabbit hole of doubting away from Jesus instead of leaning into Him in our doubt.

Questions are not a bad thing. The distinction in the direction of the questions changes everything. It all comes down to how we lean in our questioning. On the one hand, we can lean into Jesus! Lean into who we know Him to be! Remember the miracles! Remember the answered prayers! Remember the observations! Remember the words

He has said. Hopefully, this story shows you that He cares about your questions. Lean into Him.

The other option amid doubt or questions is to lean away from Jesus. Forgetting the miracles! Forgetting what He has done! Forgetting what has been seen! Forgetting who He is! Forgetting what He has said. Forgetting the community He has given us to help in the middle of doubt and lead us back to the truth! Isolation is a scary place. It can open us to vulnerability. It can leave us with only ourselves to answer the questions. It can lead to chaos and confusion, making it much harder to get out of the dark and see the light.

Thank you, Thomas, for your honesty! Thank you for your boldness and your loyalty! Thank you for your authenticity. Think about the stories in the divinely inspired word of God! Consider the grace of having Thomas' story to read in moments of doubt! Look at how God is providing in each moment! Is it encouragement through the Bible? Is He providing through words from trusted friends? Look with eyes wide open. In his moment of doubt and hopelessness, Thomas did not listen to the hope provided by His trusted friends. He was not there to witness the resurrected Jesus with His friends and characteristically stuck to his belief until proof was given. Fight the urge to doubt in isolation! Seek Jesus, seek the word, seek community, seek friends, seek a mentor. Don't doubt alone.

Jesus' response to Thomas is beautiful. Thomas' story is a reminder that Jesus welcomes our honesty. After all, He desires a genuine relationship with each of us. Jesus met Thomas in his doubt in an intentional way. He showed him the evidence he was looking for in His nail-scarred flesh. He did not judge Thomas; He met Thomas where he was at. So ask your questions, and be honest; Jesus is not afraid of your honesty. The answer may not come in nail-scarred hands and touching a scarred side. However, we can rely on the fact that the power of what those scars represent will never fade. Remember the detail of Jesus' scars. Jesus' resurrected, glorified body in Thomas' story had scars. As Christians, we can look forward to our perfected heavenly bodies: no ailments, no pain, no tears, no scars. But Jesus is revealing scars to Thomas. The scars placed on Him as He sacrificed His life for ours. Those scars represent His love for us. Those scars represent amazing grace. Those scars represent eternal life that we can only find in Him.

So, how does Thomas' story end? He could have felt like a failure. He could have thought he was past the point of no return and stayed stuck in fear and doubt. Instead, we continue to hear about Thomas in scripture. He joined back with his friends. We see him fishing with Peter (John 21) and hear his name mentioned among the apostles in Acts 1. Doubt would not be the last word of his story. It is thought that Thomas would go on to be a missionary in India and go as far as to be a martyr for Jesus! He did not let that one moment define him or stop him from following Jesus' call on his life. Neither should we!

The story's sum comes down to a question of belief. To believe or not to believe is still the question. Do we believe the word of God? Do we believe in the unconditional love of Jesus? Do we trust that He died a painful death so we might have eternal life? Do we believe it's all about Jesus' one work that paid it all, giving life incredible worth? Do we believe the miracles that we read about in scripture? Do we believe the miracles we still see today? Jesus' resurrected body was seen by more than just his closest friends. There were many eyewitnesses. Many of those closest to Jesus, including Thomas, died as martyrs for what they believed. Why would anyone die for a fake resurrection? If it wasn't true, three years of life may have seemed like a waste, but it would be much easier to disperse and return to life before Jesus. That's not what happened. Their lives centered on Jesus. They preached the gospel of Jesus. Their lives were lived for Jesus, and many of their deaths were in the name of Jesus. They believed wholeheartedly! Thomas included!

The Backstory

When I wrote this poem, it was April 2020. Like many others, I had some questions. Just mentioning that year can pull those of us who went through the global pandemic right back to that shared moment in time. If you lived it, you know. If you've heard about it, you know. There was confusion and isolation on a global scale. There were questions about safety and health, and surrounding those questions were uncertainty and even fear.

During this time, amongst the global chaos, there was about a month when people I knew passed away weekly. Walking through this time in isolation—and trying to support those close to me who were also suffering was horrible. In this season, I wrestled with questions about loss and suffering. Simultaneously, my reading brought me to Thomas' story. Before this, he was just the guy who doubted, or so I thought, but perhaps he and I had a divine appointment.

In the crux and crevices of this short but powerful story, I learned from Thomas. I realized that Thomas was not there when Jesus arrived in the locked room where many of Thomas' friends were. Question! Was he isolating himself? I began to think of the crippling power of isolation. When we went into isolation in 2020, it was hard to feel any sense of community. We couldn't easily visit a friend in need, sit and have coffee, or visit those sick. We were left with extended time away from one another, sitting in our questions—and, at times, even allowing fear to gain traction in our hearts and minds. Wherever Thomas was, he initially was not with his friends to see Jesus face to face, and the circumstances of the past week outweighed the truth his trusted friends were bringing to him.

This moment with Thomas is a story of honest doubt met with the incredible intention of Jesus. All hope had been lost for this loyal friend of Jesus. His friend and leader was dead, or so he thought. The truth is that Jesus was (and still is) fully alive. This truth did not change based on Thomas' belief, but Thomas changed because he believed in the risen savior of the world—Jesus the Messiah, "My Lord and my God!"

The Scene Study

- Write a character description for Thomas. Be detailed and use adjectives.

- What is something new you have learned about Thomas?

- What can we learn from Thomas as we experience doubt?

- How do you see Jesus' intentionality?

The Senses

- Take some time to lean into the arms of Jesus! You may not be in a season of doubt, but isn't it wonderful that we are welcome in his arms any time? Find some rocks. On the rocks, take time to paint or write your cares, your worries, your doubts, your joys, your fears, your blessings, your prayers, or maybe a name you have given yourself. You can write words or paint images. As you paint, write, draw.... Pray over what you are displaying on the rocks. Don't rush! Spend time leaning into Jesus! When you have done this, move to the following prompt. Don't rush! Take your time!

- From there, cast these rocks. Perhaps you throw them back into nature. Perhaps you cast them into the water. You could lay them at the feet of a tree or by a flower. Notice the movement as you cast them. You have to lean in to place them forward. After you cast your rock, reflect on what it means to lean into Jesus!

- Think of what it means to cast something. Casting your cares would mean a literal forward motion toward Jesus. Holding onto our cares would require movement away from Jesus, a hardness of embracing, clutching them tightly as we carry that burden on our own. Be honest with Jesus! Lean into Him.

- Reflect on who Jesus is! Who does scripture say that He is? Remember! Pray and thank Him for who He is in your life.

Chapter XII

The Criminal

The Scripture

L uke 23:32 - 43 (CSB)

32 Two others—criminals—were also led away to be executed with him. 33 When they arrived at the place called The Skull, they crucified him there, along with the criminals, one on the right and one on the left. 34 Then Jesus said, "Father, forgive them, because they do not know what they are doing." And they divided his clothes and cast lots. 35 The people stood watching, and even the leaders were scoffing: "He saved others; let him save himself if this is God's Messiah, the Chosen One!" 36 The soldiers also mocked him. They came offering him sour wine 37 and said, "If you are the king of the Jews, save yourself!" 38 An inscription was above him: This Is the King of the Jews. 39 Then one of the criminals hanging there began to yell insults at him: "Aren't you the Messiah? Save yourself and us!" 40 But the other answered, rebuking him: "Don't you even fear God, since you are undergoing the same punishment? 41 We are punished justly because we're getting back what we deserve for the things we did, but this man has done nothing wrong."42 Then he said, "Jesus, remember me when you come into your kingdom."43 And he said to him, "Truly I tell you, today you will be with me in paradise."

At Rise

The day was marked by death—the judgment, execution. The method was a cross. The moment was far from quiet and private. The celebration of the Passover holiday had passed, but the city of Jerusalem was filled with people due to the holiday. As others just finished celebrating, two criminals await their fate. I recently went to the prison cell where Paul was thought to be imprisoned in Rome, and while this is not the same location these two criminals were experiencing, the cell was created by the same ruling government. If their prison cell was anything like the one I visited, it would be cold, dark, and hopeless.

There was no natural light available in the small space. I would imagine that prisoners would have lost track of day and night in the endless dark as all hope for their futures slowly faded away.

These two criminals were eventually escorted to a place called Golgotha, meaning "the Skull," to die excruciatingly painful deaths. Gathered to watch the man between them die are religious leaders scoffing, the followers who stayed crying, and a crowd of others joining in on the yelling and mocking. It was a brutal day, and the people were out for blood. Incredibly enough, the blood they sought was the same blood that could set them free.

The Scene

Criminal.
That's all that's left of me.
Death is my destiny.
My crimes my identity.
It's done.
Decided.
Everything has caught up with me.

How ironic.
This week was meant for celebration,
Our people's deliverance.
Surely, I have done my penance.

Death can't be my sentence.
Where's my deliverance?

What if I pay back every expense?
Just pardon me.
Give me a second chance.
Wait, he's the one you're giving a second chance?
Pardoned, proclaimed with innocence.
In comparison, it makes no sense.

Are your hearts callous?
Perhaps you just think he's zealous.
An insurrectionist to save us.
And what about this other guy, Jesus?
You would take murderous over blasphemous?
He says He has come to save us,
But I guess you want what Barabas offers us.

Then they gave me my cross.
How cruel.
Forced to carry my own death tool.
As I lifted my cross,
I looked across,
My eyes met the eyes of the one they called blasphemous.
Covered in His own blood.
Thorns piercing His head.
He's so badly beaten.
How is He not already dead?

Before there was anything I could say,
They pushed us.

Pointed the way.

It's settled.

Today was my judgment day.

The verdict,

Guilty.

My life is how I'll pay.

A rebel,

Criminal,

That's all you see.

Let's see what would happen if you were in this judgment seat.

Suppose you switched places with me.

You wouldn't dare act so piously.

But before I could say any words at all.

Before I knew it,

We were at the place called the Skull.

Pushed to the cross to lay.

Fighting my last fight.

No!

There has to be another way.

From the corner of my eye,

That man...

He willingly lay.

Say something!!!

Anything!

If you have any power, now's the time.

Unleash everything!

AHHH!

The pain,

As the nail pierced one hand.
Unless you've felt it, you can't comprehend.
AHHH!
Is this pain alone not judgment enough?
I'm not the only one here who has messed up.
AHHH!
The final nail to keep me there,
As I lay on the cross, exposed, bare.
Now, all anyone could do was just stare.

Why are you here to watch me die?
Is there no ounce of mercy in your eyes?
To my left is the other rebel, just like me.
But between us is that man,
Also nailed to a tree.
Above him an inscription,
"Jesus, King of the Jews".

The people just keep mocking Him.
Spitting on Him.
Their anger made my crimes look like nothing in comparison.
So I decide to join in on the heckling.
What have I got to lose?
Nothing!
But maybe I'll gain something.
If you're going to prove anything
Now's the time.
Make good on all the things.
Save us now.
Destroy everything.
Start your rebuilding.

Don't just lay there.

If you are the king,

Prove it!

Get us down from these trees.

Start fighting!

Prove something!

Anything!

Ahh!

Give this pain a final ending!

But all He did was nothing.

And then I heard something.

Yes, come on, speak!

Say Something!

Anything!

But these words were not what I was Expecting.

"Father, Forgive them, for they know not what they are doing."

What Am I hearing?

How is His response loving?

It's beyond my understanding.

Wait!

No,

I turn to look at Him and in a moment realize.

No! It can't be?

But it's so plain to see.

The truth is right in front of my eyes.

I am utterly horrified.

Why?

It's next to the Messiah that I've been crucified

It's like He's a sacrifice.

Suddenly, I am aware of my humanity.

I deserve all of this in reality.

But He,

I know now that He is who He claims to be.

Messiah.

King of Kings.

Dying next to me,

In full humility.

How can this be?

So I plead!

Quiet!

Everyone!

Please.

Just let Him be.

He is innocent!

I look to the other rebel, the one like me.

How can you not see?

He is nothing like you and me.

He shouldn't be here.

He should be free.

He is praiseworthy.

But no one listens.

They see what they want to see.

I just look at him.

I can't believe what is happening.

This death, I know I am deserving.

But not Him.

We've waited for you.

And now we've nailed you to a cross.

How can this be?

How did we not see?

And though I know I don't deserve it.

I have one last brave moment.

As I struggle to get a breath.

I make my statement.

I need Him to know that I believe.

So I ask,

Simply,

"Jesus, remember me...?"

I know I don't deserve mercy.

But I have to let Him know that I see.

Then, unexpectedly,

He says to me.

"Today, in paradise with me, you will be."

And I know instantly.

Through His eyes of mercy,

That it would be exactly as He had said it would be.

I don't deserve this kind of grace and mercy.

Yet He gave it to me freely.

For my sin, His blood now intercedes.

He is on that cross for me.

All I had to do was believe.

The Story

The scene is a paradox. Innocence takes on guilt so that the guilty can be found innocent. The sacrificial ransom Jesus paid for us would be excruciatingly painful. Crucifixion is a slow, painful execution, giving these two men time. Time to observe the crowd. Time to observe the circumstances. Time to observe this man, Jesus. Where would these guilty men find themselves amongst this mixed crowd of Roman soldiers, religious leaders, grieving followers, and those who stood there and mocked Him? At one point, they both joined in on the mocking. (Matthew 27:44). Perhaps they were taunting to rile Jesus up in a last-ditch effort to save themselves. Jesus' popularity at this time was great, so most likely, these men had heard of him before this moment. Perhaps they were just joining in on the bandwagon. Who knows what motivated these men to join in on the insults, but they did.

Then, there was a split in the comradery of these two criminals. One man had a divine realization as they spent time next to Jesus. Amidst the pain of the wounds, the difficulty to breathe, the humiliation of public execution, and the hours that passed, one man recognized that the man next to him was not only innocent, but He was the king, just like the inscription said. This criminal would have been of Jewish descent, so he would have known about the promised one. Imagine this moment as he tried to stop the other man from furthering the insults and recognized his humanity next to Jesus' royalty, and though he might not have entirely understood it fully in this exact moment, Jesus' deity. Perhaps he recalled stories and prophecies. (Isaiah 53:12)

There is no way of knowing precisely what happened to cause this man to realize the truth about who Jesus was. Just enough is written in the Gospel of Luke to graciously reveal the magnitude of what was occurring. Jesus died on the cross for ALL! Not one group of people, not the holiest, not the quote-on-quote good (in reality, how can we measure what good enough even is?). He died for all, once and for all! The perfect sacrifice to take away our sins. All it takes is one moment with Jesus to change everything, and this criminal's story, graciously provided in scripture, gives us that example. Jesus did not tell him to pray, be baptized, and then you will be with me in paradise. Jesus did not say to turn ten people to Him, and then you will be with me in paradise. Jesus did not say you've done a lot of bad things; let's try and count those things up. Now, do as many good things as possible to compensate for those bad things, and maybe you will be with me in paradise. Jesus did not say; it's too late; you are too far gone for me. NO! Jesus, from the cross, said, "Today you will be with me in paradise" (Luke 23:43 CSB). The criminal's encounter on the cross with Jesus reveals that one moment with Jesus changes everything instantly. It also uncovers the depths of Christ's love and the fact that, in all reality, it is not about what we do; it is all about what Christ did for us. It seems too simple, I know. It feels like we should have to pay Him back, but we never could. All we have to do is believe, just like this criminal.

The story of the criminal points us to a remarkable fact, the thing that sets following Jesus apart from any other belief system. It is all about Jesus, not all about us. Sure, our response matters—these criminals are prime examples of two varying responses to Him—but ultimately, it is about choosing to trust in what He did for us, not what we can do for Him. It is not about the work we do; it is all about the one work He did!

My friend, you are so precious to Jesus that he came humbly as a baby, lived a life, died a criminal's death, and then rose again, conquering sin and death. You are so precious to Him that He paid the ransom for all our sins—why? Because He loves us. Remember that conversation early on with Nicodemus?

16 For God loved the world in this way: He gave his one and only Son, so that everyone who believes in him will not perish but have eternal life. (John 3:16 CSB)

The Bible is the great Love story of God. Since the fall of humanity and the moment sin entered the world, God set His plan of redemption in place. In Genesis 3:21, we see God cover the shame of Adam and Eve with a temporary covering, demonstrating His grace even then. This story shows Jesus' permanent covering for our sins through his blood on the cross. Grace is not getting what we deserve. The criminals deserved punishment, but in the end, the one man got what he did not deserve: eternal salvation, eternal life, forgiveness, and redemption. Why? Because he believed. The same is true for all of us. We deserve punishment for our sins, but when we believe in Jesus, we receive life eternal with Him.

This story represents the ultimate choice. Do I believe in Jesus? Or do I continue on my own? Each person is found in the dichotomy of the two criminals. Guilty of sin, with the choice, rejection, or re-demption. How gracious that even on a deathbed, someone still has time to believe. If there is breath, there is time. This story provides that example. There is also beauty and grace in a life of belief. We often think of eternal life as the end goal; don't get me wrong, eternal life in Heaven with Jesus will be incredible. It is the believer's true home. But we don't have to wait to start living an abundant life in Him. Life with Jesus begins when we believe. That does not mean life will be free of pain or trials, but life in Jesus has hope. Life in Jesus has a purpose beyond ourselves. Life in Jesus is abundant. Life in Jesus means He is there in the joy and the trials. The very last words recorded from Jesus to His followers before ascending are "....and remember I am with you always" (Matthew 28:20 CSB). What an incredible promise. Ultimately, there are two roads—one with Jesus and one rejecting Jesus. It is an individual choice to make.

The Backstory

Writing this spoken word completely wrecked me. Why? Writing this chapter meant thinking through the eyes of a criminal on the cross next to Jesus. Writing from this criminal's perspective required imagining the pain, imagining the shame, imagining the humiliation, and yet, Jesus endured that same pain and endured the same shame of the same execution. Writing from this criminal's perspective required thinking through the mocking words of the crowd. Writing from the perspective of this criminal meant recognizing innocence through the eyes of guilt. Writing from this criminal's perspective, I began to see myself in him because my sins equally nailed Jesus to the cross. This reality breaks me.

I thought of the eyes of the guilty criminal looking into the eyes of the innocent Jesus. I felt the weight of what Jesus did for every one of us. I realized that I am no better than that criminal on the cross. My sin put him on the cross just as much as the sin of the one dying next to Him. The innocence of Jesus on that day took on my guilt. He took the punishment I deserved. Sin is sin, and I am guilty and undeniably in need of a savior, just like the criminal that was next to Him. Romans 3:23 (CSB), "For all have sinned and fall short of the glory of God." We are all deserving of punishment, yet Jesus' sacrifice on the cross provides redemption for ALL who BELIEVE. The two criminals on the cross provide a powerful depiction of two roads. Two decisions. This story squashes all self-righteousness because we are all guilty. With tears running down my face, this story revealed the magnitude of Jesus' grace in a mighty way. As you read this story, embrace the power of Jesus' love for you. I hope you recognize Him for who He is and what He came to do for you.

The Scene Study

- Imagine the moment this man finally understood who Jesus is. Reflect on what he might have felt, thought, and seen.

- How do you see grace in this story? What was deserved, and what was given?

- Imagine the scene with all of the varying opinions and emotions. Some are grieving, some are bloodthirsty, some are mocking, and some are there as executioners and law enforcers. Describe it as if you were an eyewitness reporter.

- What can we learn from the two responses from the two criminals?

The Senses

- Find a quiet place. Make the space intentional, whether in nature or inside. Reflect on the magnitude of God's agape love. Write about it and what it means to you. Be specific. Take some time today, whether you believe or are still processing, to write a thank you letter to Jesus. Find a quiet place and ponder the beauty of His grace. Think of the reality of the cross. Absorb the beauty of that horrific day as innocent blood was given to take on the guilt of the world. Take time to reflect and respond in a letter to Jesus.

• Lastly, if you have never stopped and said, "I believe in Jesus," I encourage you to make today that day. One moment with Jesus changes everything. This does not mean things get easier or better in this physical life. The thief on the cross did not suddenly come down from the cross, but he would be with Jesus in paradise eternally. We have all sinned. We all need a savior. Jesus came to this earth to redeem humanity once and for all. His one act on the cross conquered sin, but the rest of the story also conquers death. Three days after his death, Jesus miraculously rose from the grave. There are many eyewitness accounts of this. His resurrection is not simply a myth or fairytale. If you proclaimed your belief in Jesus today in a private spot, I encourage you to share it with a friend who is a believer or find a church to share with you in this celebration and be there to walk with you on this journey.

The Epilogue

I wish I could sit in on every small group or across from each individual to chat through these stories over a cup of coffee. But since I can't do that, you can still grab that coffee if you'd like. I'd love to share from my heart for a few minutes.

Today, I was talking with my friend and editor. Our talks concerning each chapter led us into rich, deep, and beautiful conversations centered around the artistry of this book, but even more the theology and impact of these stories—the impact of Jesus. Today, much of our time was focused on the choices within these stories. Will I accept Jesus? Or will I take a false savior that the world offers me? This is still a daily choice—no matter how long and sincerely we have followed Jesus. It is the choice I was led to present you with through these stories over and over again. Will we choose lies, or will we choose truth? Will we choose fear, or will we choose love? Will we choose death, or will we choose life? Will we choose the world, or will we choose Jesus?

I hope that your relationship with Jesus has deepened. For me, this journey of writing a book has brought the grace of Jesus to life in an incredible way. The detail and intentionality He took in each of these encounters pointed me to His character and care. I went to church tonight, and the minute the worship music started, I began to cry, and the floodgates did not close through the entire worship set. As we sang about His faithfulness, I thought of these stories and was overwhelmed by who Jesus is—how, no matter how hard I try, His grace, love, and faithfulness are more incredible than I can ever comprehend.

Throughout the entirety of this writing process, the phrase I continued to say over and over again was: It feels like God is pouring into me. The stories were coming to life in new ways. Not because they were different than before but because little phrases, minor details, and the background to the stories were revealed as I read, researched, and wrote. As I then began to write, it simply felt like an overflow. What God had poured in was now simply being poured back out. These people I had read about for years felt more like real people than ever because I had spent time with their stories, time getting to know them more fully. The impact of Jesus in their lives began to impact my life. Writing these twelve chapters reminded me of what I always knew. While I get to read the end of these stories and know who Jesus was then and still is now, these individuals were real people, living real stories, going through real experiences. I sincerely hope they came to life in a new, fresh, and real way for you as well. Ultimately, I hope that Jesus, and who He is, came to life for you in a tangible and beautiful way.

So, as you put the pages of this book down for now, I hope you are reminded that the Word of God is active. What does that mean? This means that we can continue learning from these stories that occurred

2,000 years ago. It means that when you read a story and it is in the perfect timing and comforts you, or guides you, it is because it is God's word. Reading it can almost feel like a conversation with Him. It means you can learn new things, and God can reveal new parts you may not have realized even after years of studying. So, I hope you continue to dive into the beautiful depths of scripture. Look for newness; seek it daily.

You do not have to be a theologian to know who Jesus is. I'm just a theatre girl who felt a call to write. The writing was my time of solitude and discovery with Jesus, the Word of God, and a computer to process. But If I'm being vulnerable, I will tell you that I sometimes felt like an impostor. Who am I to think that I can write this? What qualifications do I have? But Jesus came for all. His word is for all. He broke down the barriers of needing an intermediary between us and God. I hope that the fact that He came for all has been reinforced as you've looked through these stories in scripture. So, you are not an imposter; you are a cherished individual.

I don't know if you read this book in a small group, on your own, or perhaps even with a performance in mind. If by chance you read alone, I encourage you to talk with a friend. Reflect and share; it does not have to be these stories, but be in community. Even in just twelve stories, we saw the importance and continued talk of disciples. Jesus had a following, and then He had His inner circle of twelve. He exemplifies the importance of community. What happens in the community? Well, again, let me share a little. The importance of accuracy to the Bible was of the highest priority. So, I chose an editor I knew and trusted with a seminary background. I wanted to know that if I was sending this out to the world, that it had been checked. The result was some of the most profound conversations surrounding these stories, the stories that surrounded the stories, and the depths of the details. In a community, we can learn and grow with each other.

As our coffee chat ends, I hope you leave with a renewed desire to seek Jesus and know Him more.

Blessings

Angela

The Journal

—

Connect With Angela

Let's collaborate! Angela would love to collaborate on creatively telling stories for God's glory. Connect with her to bring these stories to life at your church or event as a performance or as a speaker.

Visit www.angela-oneill.com to start the conversation.

www.ingramcontent.com/pod-product-compliance
Lightning Source LLC
Chambersburg PA
CBHW062051080426
42734CB00012B/2608